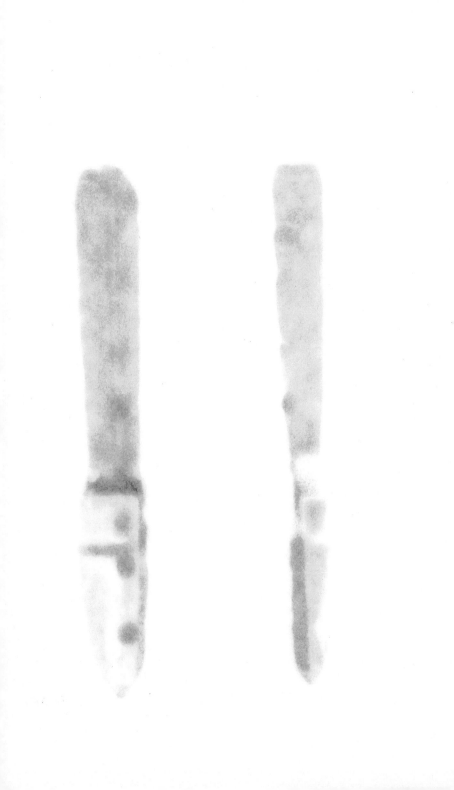

Twelve English Statesmen

HENRY THE SEVENTH

HENRY THE SEVENTH

BY

JAMES GAIRDNER

MACMILLAN AND CO., LIMITED
ST. MARTIN'S STREET, LONDON

1926

Republished by
Scholarly Press, 22929 Industrial East, St. Clair Shores, Michigan 48080

Standard Book Number 403-00020-3

This edition is printed on a high-quality,
acid-free paper that meets specification
requirements for fine book paper referred
to as "300-year" paper

CONTENTS

CHAPTER I

CHAPTER I

EARLY LIFE

NEVER was king so thoroughly disciplined by adversity before he came to the throne as was King Henry VII. Without a father even from his birth, driven abroad in his childhood owing to the attainder of his family, more than once nearly delivered up to his enemies and owing life and liberty to his own and his friends' astuteness, his ultimate conquest of the Crown was scarcely so much a triumph of ambition as the achievement of personal safety. He could not help his birth, and in spite of the imperfections in his title he could not help being regarded as head of the House of Lancaster after Henry VI. and his son had been cut off. He could not help, in short, being an object of suspicion and jealousy to Edward IV. and Richard III. successively, even if he had made no effort to dispossess them of the throne; and, in truth, against Edward he seems to have done nothing for his own part, though the Earl of Oxford's expedition to St. Michael's Mount must have been with a view to advance his claims. He might, indeed, for anything we know to the contrary, have remained an exile and a refugee to the end of his days, had not the tyranny of Richard III. drawn towards

him the sympathies of Englishmen in a way they were
not drawn towards him during Edward's reign.

It was through his mother that he derived his claim
to the Crown ; for though his father traced his descent
from Cadwallader, and the Welsh were pleased with his
pedigree, it was only spoken of when he came to the
throne as conferring some additional lustre on his title.
Nor could the fact that his paternal grandfather, Sir
Owen Tudor, a simple knight of Wales, was bold enough
to marry the widow of Henry V., daughter to Charles
VI. of France, in any way advance his pretensions,
though it made his father a half-brother to Henry VI.
and allied him besides with the royal family of France.
But standing as he did in such close relations with the
king, Edmund Tudor, the son of Sir Owen by the
Queen-dowager Katharine, was raised by Henry VI. to
the dignity of Earl of Richmond ; and the title of
course descended to Henry, who was his only son. This
was all that he could claim by right of his father.

But his mother, Margaret Beaufort, only daughter of
John Beaufort, Duke of Somerset, was the lineal heiress
of John of Gaunt. It is true that her grandfather, John
de Beaufort, was only a natural son, born before his
father's, John of Gaunt's, marriage with his mother,
Katharine Swynford. But the Beauforts had been
legitimated by Act of Parliament in the reign of Richard
II., and though a reservation of the royal dignity was
introduced into the patent when it was confirmed by
Henry IV., it is now well known that there was no such
exception in the original grant or in the Act of Parliament of Richard II.'s time. So that, failing the issue of
John of Gaunt by his two previous marriages, his de-

scendants by Katharine Swynford, even by sons whom she bore him before marriage, were the true representatives of the House of Lancaster, and could claim the throne itself if that House had any claim to it at all.

It is by no means certain, however, that Henry knew he had this advantage, and the silence of the Act of Parliament declaring his right to the Crown, as to its true hereditary character, seems rather to imply that the ground was not thought safe. No doubt there was another reason for reticence in the fact that the assertion of Henry's own hereditary claim would have discredited that of his wife as heiress of the House of York, and alienated his Yorkist supporters. But it seems probable, in the nature of things, that the reservation inserted by Henry IV. in the original patent of Richard II. was regarded as a true legal obstacle which it was better simply to ignore than expressly to overrule it in the parliamentary confirmation of Henry's title.

Such, then, was the nature of Henry's ancestral claims. We come now to his personal history. He was born at Pembroke Castle on the feast of St. Agnes the Second (28th January) 1457. In after years, when he was king, his mother dated a letter to him, "At Calais town thys day of Seynt Annes, that y dyd bryng ynto thys world my good and gracyous prynce, kynge and only beloved son." *St. Anne's* day falls in July; but we have ample evidence that Henry was born in the beginning of the year, and that "Seynt Annes" means St. Agnes. The circumstances of his birth were peculiar. His father was already more than two months dead, and his mother, incredible as the fact may seem, was only fourteen years old—in fact, had not quite completed her

fourteenth year—when the event occurred. At least
this was distinctly stated in her own and her son King
Henry's presence in a set speech delivered by Bishop
Fisher at Cambridge as Chancellor of the University,
so that its truth can hardly be questioned. The orator
added, "And she, as we perceive, is not a woman of
great stature." The birth was probably not unattended
with danger to the sole living parent, and her very early
maternity no doubt interfered with her growth.

Pembroke Castle, in which Henry was born, was the
property of his uncle, Jasper Tudor, Earl of Pembroke.
It is an imposing ruin at this day—wonderfully perfect
still, in spite of the battering Oliver Cromwell gave it—
and is thus described by the antiquary Leland, who
visited it in Henry VIII.'s reign: "The Castel stondith
hard by the waul (the town wall) on a hard rokke and
is veri larg and strong, being doble wardid. In the uttei
ward I saw the chaumbre wher King Henri the VII.
was borne, in knowlege wherof a chymmeney is new
made with the armes and badges of King Henri the
VII." In this strong fortress, while England was con-
vulsed with civil war, the child and his mother remained
in tolerable security under the protection of his uncle
Jasper; and even after Jasper was attainted as a Lancastrian, when Edward IV. obtained the Crown, young
Henry being then four years old, both this and other
fortresses for some time held out against the conquerors.
But not for many years; for even Harlech surrendered
in 1468, and it was the last stronghold that remained
in Lancastrian hands. And it was doubtless in Harlech
Castle, though our informant does not give the name of
the fortress, that young Henry was at length besieged

when the place fell into the hands of the victorious Yorkists, and he found himself a prisoner among strangers.

The winner of Harlech Castle was William, Lord
Herbert, who had been created a peer by Edward IV.
at his coronation, in recognition of his staunch devotion
to the House of York. Just after this achievement he
was advanced to the title of Earl of Pembroke, forfeited
by the attainder of Henry's uncle, Jasper. And that it
was into his hands that young Henry fell by the fortune
of war we may look upon as certain, for in his hands we
actually find him not long after. On the 16th of July
1468 the new Earl of Pembroke made his will, in one
part of which he says: "I will that Maud my daughter
be wedded to the Lord Henry of Richmond." He thus
exercised the rights of a feudal guardian over an unfor-
tunate lad who was now parted from his own relations.
Harlech Castle, built upon a steep rock overhanging
the sea in those days (though a mile of sand has since
accumulated between it and the shore), had been supposed impregnable, and must have appeared the safest
place in which the young earl could be kept. It was
also the key of the country, and just before its capture
Earl Jasper had been holding "many sessions and 'sizes
in King Harry's name" throughout Wales. The castle,
however, surrendered by composition, under what circumstances we do not quite know. Young Henry became a
prisoner and his uncle was now an attainted refugee.

His new guardian, we see, had the most friendly
intentions towards him, and though he was now only
eleven years old, the match would probably have taken
effect in due time but for further disturbances. But
his new guardian was put to death in the following

year by the insurgents under Robin of Redesdale, and in the year after that Edward IV. was driven out of his kingdom and Henry VI. restored. Nevertheless, during the brief interval between the death of her husband and the restoration of King Henry, Maud, Countess-dowager of Pembroke, continued to take care of the young lad's education and brought him up in her family. He had, of course, received the rudiments of scholarship already from teachers appointed by his mother and his uncle Jasper. His health had been delicate from childhood, and while he could be safely moved about in Wales, he was frequently sent from one place to another, under the care of sagacious tutors, merely for change of air. One of these tutors, by name Andreas Scotus, in after years at Oxford reported to Henry's biographer and poet-laureate, Bernard André, that he had never seen a boy who exhibited so much quickness in learning.

On the restoration of Henry VI. in 1470 his uncle Jasper took him again out of the hands of the Countess Maud and brought him up to London. He there presented him to King Henry, who, it is said, being much struck with the boy's "wit and likely towardness" (he was then in his fourteenth year), could not refrain from remarking to those about him, "Lo, surely, this is he to whom both we and our adversaries shall hereafter give place." Prophecies of this sort, no doubt, are seldom recorded until they have been accomplished; and it must be observed that if King Henry uttered it just as it is recorded, he could have had little confidence in the future of his then living son, who was more than three years Henry Tudor's senior. But it is conceivable that, looking at a bright and clever boy, he might have

said something as to the possibility of his one day
winning a kingdom. The saying, however, took its
place in more than one contemporary history as a prophecy, and is embalmed accordingly in the third part
of Shakespeare's *Henry VI.*[1]

Fortune, however, soon changed again. Edward IV.
recovered his throne in the spring of next year. Margaret of Anjou and her son the prince only reached
England the day Warwick was defeated and slain at
Barnet, and they were finally defeated themselves a
month later at Tewkesbury. All was then lost for the
House of Lancaster. The prince was killed on the field
—but apparently after the battle, not in it. His unhappy father, Henry VI., was a few days later put to
death within the Tower. The civil war had already
made politicians quite unscrupulous, and there was now
no direct issue of the line of John of Gaunt remaining
except the descendants of Katharine Swynford. Nor
could there have been much immediate danger to the
House of York from such a stripling as the Earl of
Richmond, now little more than fourteen years old,
even if there had not been some apparent defect in his
title. Nevertheless it was clear now that he could
no longer remain safely even in Wales ; and his uncle
Jasper took him across the sea, hoping to find an asylum
for him in France. The wind, however, carried them
into Britanny, then an independent duchy; and the
duke, Francis II., received them with great satisfaction,
knowing well the value of such political refugees if he
should require the assistance of England against his
powerful neighbour France.

[1] Act IV. sc. vi.

It was at the urgent request of his mother, the Countess of Richmond, that Henry was thus conveyed abroad. She, however, remained in England, having probably before this time married her second husband, Henry, Lord Stafford, the son of the Duke of Buckingham. She, at least, was not an object of jealousy to Edward IV., who endowed her with lands in Devonshire, where it is supposed that she chiefly lived. But he made pretty persistent efforts to induce the Duke of Britanny to give up her son to him, urging that he intended not to treat him as a prisoner, but to marry him to one of his own daughters; so that at last Duke Francis delivered him up to an English embassy, which carried him as far as St. Malo, where they were about to have taken ship for England. Henry believed that he was going to his death, and, in the words of the old chronicler, "for very pensiveness and inward thought fell into a fervent and sore ague." But Jean du Quelenec, Admiral of Britanny, an old and faithful councillor of the duke, took alarm at what seemed to him like a stain upon his master's honour, and persuaded him at the last moment to stay the effect of his weak concession. Pierre Landois, the duke's treasurer, was despatched to St. Malo to intercept the embassy, to whom he made some plausible excuses for his coming, and detained them in conversation, while his men, unknown to them, got the earl conveyed into a sanctuary within the town; and the embassy were obliged to return to England without their prize. All that was conceded to them, in answer to their remonstrances, was a promise that since matters had taken this turn (for Landois imputed the escape solely to their own care-

!essness), the earl should be safely kept in sanctuary, or be again placed in confinement.

So Henry remained in Britanny, and was somewhat closely guarded for the remainder of Edward IV.'s reign; but it is not likely that his confinement was very severe. In 1482 his stepfather, Lord Henry Stafford, died, leaving him, as it appears, by will, "a trapper of four new horse harness of velvet"; and his mother soon afterwards married her third husband, Thomas, Lord Stanley, at this time steward of King Edward's household.

The death of Edward IV. and the usurpation of Richard III. opened the way for new projects, in which Henry was no longer to remain a passive instrument or victim of the designs of others. Richard had really paved Henry's way to the throne by usurping it himself; for it was on the plea of the illegitimacy of his brother's children that he claimed it, some time before he put the two young princes to death. And this point seems to have been clearly perceived by Richard's chief instrument, Buckingham, who, we cannot but suspect, was labouring all the while prior to the usurpation, not so much for Richard's benefit as for his own. For he, too, was a descendant of the Beauforts, and being upon the spot, probably imagined that he could seize the prize himself before his exiled cousin appeared on the scene. He had vast influence in Wales, and laid claim also to the whole inheritance of Humphrey de Bohun, Earl of Hereford, of which one half had been annexed to the Crown during the sway of the House of Lancaster and should have come to him on the death of Henry VI. And Richard seems very nearly, in addition to other acts of liberality, to have released to him the moiety of

these possessions, which had been so long detained from
him. But he had higher aspirations still; and when
Richard committed to prison as a dangerous intriguer
the astute John Morton, Bishop of Ely, Buckingham
begged that he might have his custody. This was
granted, and the duke took him down to Wales, where
he had some remarkable conversations with his prisoner,
which will be found reported in Hall's and Grafton's
Chronicles, most probably from information derived from
Morton himself.

The substance is that Buckingham simply encouraged
his prisoner to speak his mind frankly about Richard III.
and the best means of deposing him, declaring that he
himself was quite alienated from him in heart, though he
had parted from him with a pleasant countenance. He
said he perceived clearly that Richard was disliked by
the whole nobility, "so that" (as his speech is reported)
"I saw my chance as perfectly as I saw my own image
in a glass." For two days at Tewkesbury he had
dreamed about securing the Crown for himself. But he
reflected that this would certainly involve the renewal
of civil war, and that, if successful, he could only establish
his rights as a conqueror, and incur the hatred of the
whole nobility, as Richard had done. And after all, as
he confessed to Morton, it suddenly occurred to him
that he was not the true representative of the Beaufort
line, for he was only descended from Edmund, Duke of
Somerset, who was a younger brother. How he came
to overlook this rather material fact he did not inform
his prisoner, but he was very frank in stating how he
was reminded of it. "While I was in a maze," he said
to Morton—that is to say, while he was indulging in his

day-dream—"as I rode between Worcester and Bridg-
north I encountered with the Lady Margaret, Countess
of Richmond, now wife to the Lord Stanley, which is
the very daughter and sole heir to Lord John, Duke of
Somerset, my grandfather's elder brother; which was
as clean out of my mind as though I had never seen her,
so that she and her son, the Earl of Richmond, be both
bulwark and portcullis between me and the gate to enter
into the majesty royal and getting of the Crown."

The countess, looking upon Buckingham as the most
influential friend and supporter of King Richard, seized
the opportunity to ask his intercession in her son's
behalf, and prayed him, by the family ties which existed
between them, that he would urge the king to let him
return to England. She also alluded to the suggestion
made in Edward IV.'s time that her son should marry
one of that king's daughters, and said that if Richard
were agreeable to such a match, now that the issue of
Edward IV. were cut off from the succession, she herself
would be well pleased that her son should take the
young lady without any dowry. Evidently this suggestion opened the eyes of Buckingham more fully than the
mere accident of his meeting with the countess. To get
rid of King Richard and seize the Crown himself seemed
on fuller consideration a policy beset with dangers, for
on the one side he would be constantly opposed by those
who upheld the right of King Edward's daughters, while
on the other the claims of the Earl of Richmond were
undeniably superior to his own. His life as king would,
under the circumstances, have been intolerable; and if
the two rivals should make common cause against him,
the alliance being made fast by a marriage between the

earl and Edward's eldest daughter, the game was simply
at an end. All this must have passed through his mind
when the countess asked his intercession for her son, a
request which he very naturally evaded. But after their
meeting was over, when she had passed on to Worcester
and he to Shrewsbury, he set himself to recast his plan ;
and being fully resolved, at all events, to aid in dethron-
ing King Richard, he conceived that it might best be
done by that very combination which he saw would be
so fatal to himself if he, in his turn, played the part
of a usurper. He therefore informed Morton that he
would be glad to assist the Earl of Richmond to the
Crown as heir to the House of Lancaster, in whose cause
both his father and his grandfather had lost their lives,
if the earl would engage to marry Elizabeth, eldest
daughter of the late King Edward.

Bishop Morton, who had always been an adherent of
the House of Lancaster so long as there remained any
chance, in Edward IV.'s time, of vindicating their pretensions, was simply delighted to hear of the duke's
intention, and resolved that he should not be allowed
to cool in it. He at once led the duke to confer with
him as to the means of carrying out the project, and
who should be taken into confidence. Buckingham
would begin, of course, with the Lady Margaret, as she
was commonly called, the earl's mother. Morton advised him to make use of the services of her dependant,
Reginald Bray, to whom, with the duke's consent, he
wrote, urging him to come at once to Brecknock. Bray
accordingly came from Lancashire, where the messenger
found him with Lord Stanley and the countess, and to
him the design was first imparted. The duke and

Morton desired him to advise his mistress first to obtain the assent of the queen-dowager, Elizabeth Woodville, to the project, and then secretly send a message to her son in Britanny to tell him the high honour that was prepared for him if he would swear to marry Elizabeth of York. With this commission Bray was despatched, and the bishop next told the duke that if he were in his own Isle of Ely he could make many friends to further the scheme, and that the whole of that district was so well protected by nature that with four days' warning he could set Richard at defiance. This the duke well knew, but he hesitated about letting his prisoner escape, till Morton, taking the matter into his own hands, fled secretly by night in disguise. He first came to his see of Ely, where he found both money and friends, and then sailed into Flanders, where he remained, doing good service to the Earl of Richmond until the scheme devised at Brecknock had been realised and the earl had become King of England. It is needless to say that the Lady Margaret, the Countess of Richmond, entered into this scheme with the utmost satisfaction. In order to communicate with the queen-dowager, she made use of the services of a Welsh physician named Lewes, then attending upon her, who was well known among people of rank for his skill in his profession. He readily undertook a journey to Westminster in order to seek out Queen Elizabeth in the sanctuary, and get her consent to the scheme, as he could confer with her in his professional character without incurring suspicion. And he no sooner opened the project to Queen Elizabeth than she too embraced it with joy,—as might well have been anticipated. For she was really a prisoner in the

sanctuary with what remained of her family, and she
had had bitter occasion to regret having yielded to the
smooth persuasions even of men like Cardinal Bourchier,
who, thinking he might safely pledge himself, body and
soul, for the security of the young Duke of York, had
caused her to deliver that young prince into the tyrant's
power.　And now she was bereft of her two only sons,
and shut up with five daughters in a sanctuary which
was surrounded by a guard of Richard's soldiers, lest
any of them should be conveyed abroad.　But the
marriage project, if it could only be effected, would
overthrow the tyrant, release her and her children from
their present discomforts, and restore them to their true
position in the State.

So the matter was easily arranged between the two
mothers.　The next thing was to communicate with
Richmond in Britanny, for which purpose the Lady
Margaret, his mother, at first proposed to employ a
priest, named Christopher Urswick, whom she had lately
taken into her service, but considering that the plan
had originated with the Duke of Buckingham, she
ultimately chose an esquire, named Hugh Conway, as a
more dignified messenger.　The Earl of Richmond was
then a free man in Britanny, for since the death of
Edward IV. the Duke of Britanny had released him from
such restraint as he had previously put upon him ; and
Conway was to advise him to return home as soon as
possible and land in Wales, where he would be sure to
find friends.　At the same time, to make matters sure,
another messenger, named Thomas Ramme, was despatched from Kent to land in Calais while Conway
crossed the sea from Plymouth ; and both messengers

made such good speed that they arrived in the Court of Britanny within less than an hour of each other, and were able to confirm each other's message in communication with the Earl of Richmond, who soon sent them back to accelerate arrangements.

The conspiracy was now widespread, and consequently unsafe; but the confederates were trusty, and Richard, though suspicious of some things, was not aware that he was in any serious danger. It is not probable, although Polydore Vergil says so, that he seriously suspected Buckingham. But he had sent an ambassador to the Duke of Britanny ostensibly to propose a diet on commercial affairs—really to keep watch lest the duchy should be made a basis of operations against him, and to persuade the duke to put Richmond once more in confinement. The duke, however, evaded his request, and while maintaining outward friendship with King Richard, promised Henry his hearty support in his project of invasion. He was, in fact, prepossessed in his favour, and sanguine of the success of the confederacy against King Richard. For, besides Henry, there were other English refugees at his Court, among whom was Sir Edward Woodville, the queen-dowager's brother, a naval commander of whom Richard stood in dread; and having with him two such prominent leaders of English factions, quite agreed in their aims, he could hardly doubt that the usurper would speedily be dethroned. So, in spite of Richard's watchfulness, his enemies matured their project in Britanny, not only without the smallest impediment but with substantial aid and encouragement from the duke. And they arranged with their friends in England that Henry should

land somewhere on the English coast about the 18th of
October, on which day a number of simultaneous risings
had been planned to take place all over the southern
counties from Kent to Exeter, while Buckingham
on the very same day was to raise his standard at
Brecknock.

The day came, and Edward Courtenay with his brother
Piers, Bishop of Exeter, raised forces in Devonshire and
Cornwall. In Kent Richard Guildford and others did
the like, and there were risings at the same time in Berk-
shire and in Wiltshire. Maidstone, Newbury, Salisbury,
and Exeter were the four points at which a simultaneous
movement had been planned to begin over the south of
England. But the rebellion failed, more perhaps from
physical causes which it was impossible to forecast than
from the suddenly-awakened activity and watchfulness
of Richard. The inundation of the Severn—"the Duke
of Buckingham's Great Water," as it continued to be
called for a long time after—cut off the leader of the
whole movement from his allies. The Earl of Richmond's
fleet was driven by storm back upon the shores of Britanny and Normandy. King Richard took measures to
have the coasts well guarded, and himself came suddenly
from Yorkshire to Salisbury, where the Duke of Buckingham, deserted by his Welsh followers and betrayed
by a dependant, was brought before him a captive and
ordered to summary execution. Finally the Earl of
Richmond's vessel, separated from the rest of his fleet,
sighted land near the harbour of Poole. But the coast
was lined with armed men collected to resist his landing,
and Henry was not deluded by a ruse by which they
invited him to come on shore, pretending to be friends

of the Duke of Buckingham. So he hoisted sail and
again crossed the Channel to Normandy, from whence
after three days he returned by land to Britanny.

His principal adherents in England, seeing how matters
stood, contrived to escape by sea and join him in the
duchy, among whom were the Marquis of Dorset, Sir
Edward Woodville, Lord Wells, the two Courtenays above
mentioned, Sir Giles Daubeney, Sir John Bourchier, Sir
Robert Willoughby, Sir Thomas Arundel, Sir John
Cheyney and his two brothers, Sir William Berkeley
and Thomas his brother, Sir Richard Edgecombe, and
some others of less note at that time, among whom was
one Edward Poynings, afterwards knighted for his
services in war, of which and of some other doings of
his we shall have occasion to speak farther on.

CHAPTER II

So ended the first great movement in England in Henry's favour, and the first attempt of Henry himself to make good his claim to the throne. Such of his friends in England as fell into the tyrant's power were of course put to death without the least remorse. Even Sir Thomas St. Leger, who had married Richard's own sister, Anne, Duchess of Exeter, was beheaded at Exeter, where Thomas Ramme, who had carried messages between the Countess of Richmond and her son, also suffered death at the same time. But many, as we have seen, contrived to save themselves by flight, and Britanny now swarmed more than ever with English refugees; while Bishop Morton and the Countess of Richmond's chaplain, Christopher Urswick, found an asylum in Flanders, with various others, who by correspondence among themselves and with friends in England still kept alive the spirit of disaffection and the prospect of relief from tyranny.

Henry himself had no reason to be seriously discouraged. His ill success seems rather to have gained him friends upon the Continent; for as he landed in Normandy he sent to Charles VIII. of France for a passport into Britanny, and this was not only granted to him by the young king (or by the regent, Madame de Beaujeu, in his name) but money for his expenses was also freely given him by the French Council.   Meanwhile, trusting to a favourable answer to his application, he had sent his ships back to Britanny, and proceeded thither himself by land by slow journeys till his messengers returned from the French Court.   Yet he appears to have been in Britanny again at least as early as the 30th of October, on which day he gave the Duke of Britanny, at Paimpol, near Brehat, a receipt for a loan of 10,000 crowns of gold.   This may have been with a view to a new crossing of the Channel by the collected fleet, in hope of forcing a landing; for as yet the news even of Buckingham's capture could hardly have reached Britanny, and his decapitation at Salisbury only took place on the 2d of November.   But tidings soon came of that event and of the total collapse of the rebellion, and presently he heard that Dorset and other friends had also arrived in Britanny and were at Vannes.   Henry summoned them to a council at Rennes, where it was resolved to make another invasion of England on some future occasion; and on Christmas Day they all went together to Rennes Cathedral, where they pledged themselves to be true to each other and swore allegiance to Henry as if he had been already king, he for his part giving his corporal oath to marry the Princess Elizabeth after he had attained the Crown. The result of their conferences was then communicated to the Duke of Britanny with a request for further aid, which, as he had already so far committed himself, he readily granted on Henry's promise, as a prince, to repay him as soon as he had obtained the kingdom.

But with all this the Duke of Britanny, as time went on, proved a very inefficient protector. For King Richard, wisely shutting his eyes to the duke's past double-dealing, renewed his request for Henry's surrender, offering to restore the earldom of Richmond to the ducal house of Britanny, to which it had belonged till the days of Edward III., if the earl were delivered up to him. The duke's own pledges and the apparent success of Richard would probably have made it difficult to evade compliance, even if there had been no other cause. But the duke was at the time incapacitated for business by an illness that affected his mental faculties, and it fell to his unpopular minister, Pierre Landois, who had been the agent used to prevent Henry being delivered up to Edward IV., to receive the English embassy. Landois would probably have been glad to protect the earl on this occasion also. But under the circumstances he seems to have felt that he incurred a more serious responsibility by declining or evading the English de-mands than by compliance; and he was on the point of surrendering the earl to King Richard when Bishop Morton in Flanders, having heard of what was going on, sent Christopher Urswick into Britanny to give his master warning. Urswick found the earl at Vannes, and was immediately despatched by him to the Court of Charles VIII. to procure a passport into France, which he soon obtained and brought to the earl in Britanny. Henry then, having made secret inquiry as to all the byways leading from Britanny into France, requested his com-panions to go with his uncle, the Earl of Pembroke, as if to pay a visit to the duke, who was at that time, for change of air, residing on the confines of the duchy. He

privately instructed his uncle, however, as soon as they
came near the borders to conduct them by the shortest
road into France; and he himself left Vannes two days
after their departure to rejoin them in the duchy of
Anjou. No man imagined that he had left the place for
good, as there still remained about three hundred Englishmen in Vannes who knew nothing of his purpose;
but after he had gone about five miles he turned into a
wood, where he changed clothes with an attendant, and
pursued the remainder of his journey as page to his
own servant, who led the way for him and a small company till, by a zigzag route adopted to defeat pursuit,
they at length reached Angers.

Henry's flight naturally caused great perplexity to
Landois. Continuing the policy of double-dealing, he
had prepared a company of soldiers, as if for the service
of Henry in his enterprise, who were really to have
apprehended him and his followers and delivered them
to King Richard. But finding his prey escaped, he sent
horsemen galloping in all directions after the fugitive,
who, it is said, had only one hour before they arrived
passed the frontier, where they could pursue him no
farther. The duke, who was now in better health, had
thus the mortification of knowing that he or his ministers
had given serious grounds of complaint both to Richard
and to Henry; and he was extremely displeased with
Landois in consequence. Since, however, matters had
taken such a turn, he determined at once to get rid of
all further responsibility for the English fugitives, and
at the same time to convince Henry, at least, of the
sincerity of his friendship. He therefore sent for
Edward Poynings and Sir Edward Woodville, and gave

them money to conduct the other Englishmen in Britanny
to the Earl of Richmond in France.

It was a great advantage to Henry and his exiled
friends to be together under the protection of a great
power like France, with which the English usurper could
not well afford to quarrel ; and the earl, to show his gratitude, sent some of his gentlemen to the Duke of Britanny,
acknowledging that it was only by his favour and protection that he and his had been preserved from imminent danger.   He then repaired to Charles VIII. at
Langeais, upon the Loire, and after thanking him for
past favours, asked his assistance to return to England,
where the nobility, he said, were anxious for his presence
to terminate the tyranny and oppression of Richard III.
The French king, or his Council, assured him that he
would be glad to promote his enterprise and liberally
assist him ; with which encouraging answer the earl
and his friends accompanied the Court to Montargis,
and afterwards to Paris.

Meanwhile in England Richard had not only triumphed
over rebellion, but got Parliament to ratify his title ; and
the queen-dowager, seeing no relief at hand, was tempted
by a politic offer made her by the usurper to come out
of sanctuary with her daughters, for whom he promised
to provide honourable marriages, with jointures of 200
marks a year each.   This was in March 1484, and even
this was a serious blow to the earl's designs, the chief
mainstay of which was his pledge to marry the eldest of
these young ladies.   But matters some time after began
to look more serious still.   For, strange to say, the
usurper seems after a while to have won the queen-
dowager's confidence, or else she believed it to be better

policy to comply with his requests than to fulfil her
compact with the Earl of Richmond. She accordingly
wrote, at Richard's suggestion, to her son, the Marquis
of Dorset, at Paris, to abandon Henry's party and come
to England, where he would be not only pardoned but
advanced to great honour by the king; and so effectual
were her persuasions that the marquis actually stole
away from Paris at night and made for Flanders. But
Richmond and his friends prevailed on the French
Council to allow them to send in pursuit of the deserter,
whom they arrested near Compiegne and brought back
to Paris.

The defection of Dorset would have been mischievous
enough, but it was not the only way in which Henry's
prospects were endangered by the queen-dowager's
vacillation and weakness. King Richard's pledge to
provide husbands for her daughters seems to have been
given with an intention of marrying them as bastard
children, considerably below their rank; but at length,
to defeat the designs of Henry, the usurper seems
actually to have hinted that he would willingly marry
his eldest niece himself as soon as he could get rid of
the impediment of a living wife, whose days were not
likely to be protracted. She died, most conveniently for
him, on the 16th of March 1485, and alarming rumours
immediately got abroad that he was actually about to
marry the Princess Elizabeth. He was compelled by
his own councillors to repudiate the intention before the
Lord Mayor and aldermen of London, but the story got
abroad, and caused much anxiety to Henry, who was
then at Rouen, preparing to collect a fleet at Harfleur
for a new expedition against England. So greatly,

indeed, did it disconcert his plans that, looking upon a match with any of Edward's daughters as now hopeless (for it was said that the second, Cecily, was also to be married, and to a man of obscure birth), he was beginning to think of marrying a sister of Sir Walter Herbert, who was very powerful in Wales, and with this view had sent secret messages to the Earl of Northumberland, who had married another of Sir Walter's sisters, when he learned, to his great relief, that Richard had been obliged to disclaim the disgraceful design imputed to him.

Meanwhile many other things had been working in Henry's favour. The cruel punishments inflicted on many of his adherents in England had caused numbers to fly beyond sea and flock to him in Paris, among whom was Richard Fox, a priest of great learning and ability, who became from that time one of Henry's leading councillors, and was advanced by him after he became king to four successive bishoprics. Many English students at the University of Paris also swore to take part with him. James Blount, captain of Hammes Castle, near Calais, was persuaded by his prisoner, the Lancastrian Earl of Oxford, not only to set him at liberty but to accompany him to the Earl of Richmond. Sir John Fortescue, porter of Calais, also went with them. Blount had left Hammes Castle well fortified and reinforced with new soldiers, but it could not be expected to stand a siege by the neighbouring garrison of Calais, and Oxford, who, after being received with joy by Henry in Paris, was immediately sent back to rescue it, was only able to secure for the garrison honourable terms of capitulation.

The preparations made by Henry for the invasion of England were so well known that Richard took the most active measures to meet the coming danger. He not only issued proclamations against Henry and his adherents, but raised money by forced loans—a thing differing only by a shade from those unpopular "benevolences" which he had declared by Act of Parliament should no longer be enforced—caused the coasts to be guarded, sent the Princess Elizabeth to Sheriff Hutton to be out of the way, and took up his position with an army at Nottingham, in the centre of the kingdom, so as to be equally ready to meet the invader in whatever quarter he might land.

Henry determined to land in his own native district. He had received messages by one Morgan of Kidwelly, a lawyer, that Rice ap Thomas, a valiant captain of South Wales, and another, named Sir John Savage, were ready to take his part; and he had every reason to believe that his uncle, Jasper Tudor, on his reappearance in that country, would be at once greeted as Earl of Pembroke, notwithstanding his attainder. The French king had given him a body of troops, under the command of an able leader named Philibert de Shaundé, and with these and the whole body of his English followers he embarked at Harfleur on the 1st of August. With a prosperous wind he reached the coast of Wales in little more than a week, and landed at Milford Haven. He kissed the ground on landing, knelt, signed himself with the cross, and sang *Judica me, Deus, et decerne causam meam.* His own company was but 2000 men, and everything depended on the trustiness of the Welsh chieftains in the first place, to whom he issued regular

summonses to join his standard, saying that he had
come to claim the Crown of England as his right and to
dispossess the usurper Richard.   The attitude of some of
these chieftains was for a few days uncertain, but as he
advanced he met with little opposition, and when he
reached Shrewsbury his ranks were swelled by a considerable body of Welsh followers.

At his landing he had sent messages to his mother,
the Lady Margaret ; to her husband, Lord Stanley, and
his brother, Sir William ; to Sir Gilbert Talbot and other
friends, to intimate that he was in Wales and would
cross the Severn at Tewkesbury.   The position of the
Stanleys at this juncture was a little peculiar.   Richard
had all along treated them as loyal friends, and had
found it politic even to show singular toleration to the
Lady Margaret, the mother of his arch-enemy, for her
husband's sake.   Her name was not included in the
general Act of Attainder against Henry's adherents, but
a special Act was passed depriving her, indeed, of her
lands for her treason in conspiring against King Richard,
but remitting the punishment due to such a crime in
consideration of the faithful service done by her husband,
and granting him her lands for life.   Lord Stanley's services were further rewarded by some substantial grants
of the forfeited property of rebels, and he was required
to keep his wife henceforth securely in some secret
place, "without any servant or company," that she
might stir up no more intrigues.   It would almost seem
that the faithful service which, as the Act declared, Lord
Stanley "hath done and intendeth to do" consisted
more of what was expected of him in the future than of
what he actually had done for King Richard in the past.

If the usurper had treated him as an enemy he could easily have raised Lancashire and Cheshire in arms against him, as Richard himself had commissioned him to do against any invader.

We are told by Sir Thomas More that Richard not unfrequently purchased with large gifts unsteadfast friendships. Of this he could hardly himself have entertained much doubt in the case of the Stanleys; and although Lord Stanley was steward of the royal household, and his brother, Sir William Stanley, Chamberlain of North Wales, while his son, Lord Strange, was joined with both of them in the commission to lead the men of Lancashire and Cheshire against invaders, Richard certainly must have suspected long before the day of trial came that the powers he had recognised rather than conferred upon the family might easily be turned against him. As a matter of fact, North Wales, under the government of Sir William, offered the invader a benevolent neutrality, and it seemed doubtful whether the power of Lancashire and Cheshire would be actively engaged in Richard's service. The usurper, however, seems really to have been blinded in the case of some Welsh chieftains whom he expected to oppose the adventurer's progress. Welsh national sympathy, on the contrary, went with the invader as a descendant of the old British kings, and the red fiery dragon of Cadwallader accompanied him in his march through Wales. So easy, indeed, was his progress that he seems actually to have reached Shrewsbury before Richard had been informed of his landing.

Matters looked serious for the usurper. South Wales, his first line of defence, was already broken

through, and Lancashire and Cheshire might not care to
bestir themselves any more than North Wales.   Sir
William Stanley and Sir John Savage were at once proclaimed traitors, and Lord Stanley was summoned
immediately to repair to the king at Nottingham, or
send his son, Lord Strange, in his place.   Lord Strange
was sent, and then Richard intimated to his father that
his presence also would be required, as the case was
urgent.   Lord Stanley pleaded sickness, and his son,
attempting to escape, was obliged to reveal the fact that
the whole family had been in communication with the
enemy.   He, however, said his father would still join
the king's standard, and consented to remain as a hostage for his loyalty.   Lord Stanley accordingly took
care to preserve the appearance of loyalty as long as it
was possible for him to do so.

This of course disappointed Henry almost as much as
Richard ; and it seems that, full of anxious thoughts, he
one night lost himself straying alone in the rear of his
army between Lichfield and Tamworth.   He, however,
rejoined his followers in the morning, and explained his
absence as owing to a secret message from allies, who
would declare themselves at a future opportunity.   To
keep up this encouraging belief he again made an abrupt
departure, and contrived a meeting with Lord Stanley
and Sir William, in which the former explained to him
the danger his son would incur by an immediate declaration on his part.   And though Henry's army was still
greatly inferior to his enemy in numbers, he received
numerous accessions to his ranks from men who had
deserted King Richard, knowing that he held them in
distrust.

As Richard was advancing to meet him Henry took up his ground near Bosworth in Leicestershire, in a place where inferior numbers could fight to most advantage, protected by a rivulet on one side and a morass on the other. And here the decisive battle was fought in which Richard lost his life and Henry won the Crown. For some time the active assistance of Lord Stanley was not given to either party, and even Sir William Stanley, who was likewise in the neighbourhood, stood aloof, though he had been actually proclaimed a traitor by the usurper. For King Richard, on being refused the immediate aid of Lord Stanley, at once ordered Lord Strange to be beheaded; but some of his attendants procured the respite of the sanguinary order till the issue of the battle had been declared. But during the engagement both Lord Stanley and Sir William openly turned against the tyrant, the latter coming to Henry's rescue just at the moment when Richard had singled him out for a personal encounter as the shortest way to bring matters to a conclusion.

Richard had gone into the field wearing his crown. It was found after the battle by Reginald Bray, who brought it to Lord Stanley, and Lord Stanley placed it on the Earl of Richmond's head, while his men everywhere raised the cry, "King Henry! King Henry!" And the victor, at once exercising royal rights, knighted upon the field eleven of his most valiant followers, among whom were Gilbert Talbot and Rice ap Thomas.

CHAPTER III

THE crowning of Henry upon Bosworth Field, although in itself but a piece of show, was the expression of a fact which could no longer be contested. England lay at Henry's feet. The issue of the battle had already given validity to his pretensions. The tyrant was removed, and there was no other rival to contest the Crown with him. Henry was therefore already king *de facto*, but how or by what right? The niceties of law cannot be considered in the stirring times of action, but the basis of all power must be right of some kind, and no one knew so well as Henry the disadvantage of reigning with an uncertain title.

How was he king? His title was Lancastrian, and the House of Lancaster had now for many years been set aside as usurpers. Moreover, the direct line had been extinguished and some doubt rested upon the legitimacy of his own branch. He could never have won the victory as heir of the House of Lancaster if his promise to marry Elizabeth had not brought him the support of a large number of Yorkists. But a crown matrimonial was not to be thought of, even on public grounds; for if he was king only by right of his wife, "he could," as Bacon

remarks, " be but a king at courtesy," and his title would
die with her, or depend upon a parliamentary settlement
if she were removed before him. He was naturally,
therefore, led to rest his claim as much as possible on
his own inherent right, without, however, challenging
minute investigation or discrediting the title of the rival
House of York, whose heiress he was about to marry.
And having been thus crowned upon the field of battle,
he at once took upon himself the royal title without any
further ceremony to intimate his accession. Indeed, it
would appear by some evidences that he had even
assumed that title before the battle, and summoned his
Welsh subjects to his standard to enable him to wrest
his kingdom from the hands of a usurper.

His first act after the victory was to send Sir Robert
Willoughby to Sheriff Hutton in Yorkshire, the castle to
which the Princess Elizabeth had been sent by Richard's
orders to be out of the way. Here was also Edward,
Earl of Warwick, son of the unhappy Duke of Clarence,
brother of Edward IV. He was a lad of ten years old,
over whom his uncle, King Richard, had stood guardian
and whom he had once designated as heir to the Crown,
though he afterwards put him out of the succession,
perhaps from a feeling that any recognition of the claims
of the Duke of Clarence's issue would discredit his own
title as Clarence's younger brother. Henry felt that it
was just as well to make sure of the person of this lad,
whose title as a male might possibly be preferred by some
Yorkists to that of the Princess Elizabeth herself, and
ordered Willoughby to bring him up to London. The
boy accordingly came up in Willoughby's escort, and was
immediately lodged in the Tower, where he remained

for the rest of his days a prisoner. As for the Princess Elizabeth, she received directions to come up and join her future husband as soon as she conveniently could, and she very soon came, escorted by a number of noblemen and ladies. She was placed at once in the keeping of the queen-dowager, her mother.

Henry meanwhile went on by easy stages to London, where, we are told by Bacon, he made his entry on a Saturday, "as he had also obtained the victory upon a Saturday; which day of the week, first upon an observation and after upon memory and fancy, he accounted and chose as a day prosperous unto him." Bacon was not without authority for writing thus; in fact he had the seemingly excellent authority of Henry's own poet-laureate and historiographer, Bernard André. But nothing is more certain than that the battle of Bosworth was fought on a Monday, not on a Saturday, and the theory that the latter was Henry's lucky day arose, or at least was justified, only from later experience. Two great rebellions during his reign were each crushed upon a Saturday—the one at the battle of Stoke, fought on the 16th of June 1487 ; the other at the battle of Black-heath, on the 17th of June 1497—and André only began to write his History three years after the latter event ; so that it is clear he was thinking of more recent occurrences when he told his readers that the victory of Bosworth Field was gained on a Saturday. But he is right, doubtless, that Henry's entry into London was on that day of the week, when, as he informs us, he himself was present, and sung a Latin ode of his own composition to greet the conqueror. In fact a contemporary MS. says that Henry's entry took place on the 3d of September,

which was the second Saturday after the battle. It
would appear, therefore, that his progress to the capital
was slow enough—a sure sign that he was well received
in the country as he went along. He probably rested
some days at St. Albans.

Another curious error that has crept into all our
histories is also traceable, not indeed to the words of
Bernard André, but to a singular misreading of them by
one of Bacon's contemporaries. Bacon himself tells us
that though accompanied in his entry by troops of noblemen, Henry rode in a close chariot, "as one that, having
been some time an enemy to the whole State and a proscribed person, chose rather to keep state and strike
a reverence into the people than to fawn upon them."
What Bacon, however, relates as a fact is only a conjec-
ture in the pages of his contemporary Speed, who shows
us clearly on what it was grounded. Henry, according
to Speed, eschewed popular acclamations, "for that, as
Andreas saith, he entered *covertly*, meaning *belike*, in a
horse-litter or close chariot." The close chariot, then, is
a mere inference from the words of Andreas (Bernard
André) as read by Speed. But the MS. of Bernard
André does not say that Henry entered the city covertly,
but joyfully (*lœtanter*, not, as Speed quotes the word,
latenter), and the whole aspect of the matter is thus
completely changed. Henry had no fear of a good
reception by the citizens, and he was not so impolitic as
to cool their ardour by reserve on his part. He was
received by the Lord Mayor and city companies at
Shoreditch, and met, as Polydore Vergil and Hall assure
us, with a very warm and enthusiastic welcome, every
one pressing forward "gladly to touch and kiss that

victorious hand which had overcome so monstrous and
cruel a tyrant." And so he rode through the city in
triumph to St. Paul's, "where he offered his three
standards"—the first bearing the figure of St. George;
the second the red fiery dragon of Cadwallader, "beaten
upon white and green sarcenet"; the third "a dun cow,
painted upon yellow tartern." Then after orisons and
Te Deum in honour of the victory, he took up his abode
for a few days at the Bishop of London's palace.

Here he summoned a Council, in which the fulfilment
of his promise to marry Elizabeth was the principal
subject of discussion, and it is said the day was even
named. But if so, there can be little doubt that he
himself had his own views upon the subject, and was
determined, as Lord Bacon intimates, not to have the
marriage celebrated till after his coronation; nor even
then till he had held his first Parliament.

Meanwhile the citizens showed their joy by processions and pageants, after the fashion of those days. A
sum of 1000 marks had been voted to the king even
before his arrival in London as a donation, and was
doubtless presented to him by the Lord Mayor at Shoreditch, in behalf of the whole 435 persons who were there
in their scarlet and violet gowns as aldermen and as
citizens. Nor is there any reason to doubt the genuine-
ness of a loyalty which, relieved from the fear of a capri-
cious and violent tyranny, looked forward now to the
cessation of civil war. But a dark cloud soon over-
shadowed their rejoicings. A deadly pestilence called
the sweating sickness, unknown in England till that day,
although other visitations of it followed at intervals
during this and the succeeding reign, made its appearance

in the city towards the close of September. On the 11th of October the Lord Mayor died of it, and his successor, elected immediately, died of it also five days later; so that a third Lord Mayor had to be chosen to carry on the functions of the mayoralty till the 28th day of the month, when the regular year of office expired. The disease also proved fatal to six of the aldermen. It was a malady which attacked men suddenly, and ran its course in four-and-twenty hours, so that if a man survived its attack so long he was safe. But some died within a single hour of the first sensation of illness, and many in two. "At the longest," wrote Dr. Caius, who as a physician had collected all the information he could get about it, "to them that merrily dined it gave a sorrowful supper."

But suddenly as it had come, so suddenly the dreadful scourge departed. From about the 21st of September, when it first made its appearance in the city, it prevailed till near the end of October, and then disappeared. Nor did the king think it necessary to put off his coronation, which took place on the appointed day, the 30th of October. He dined the three days before with Cardinal Bourchier, Archbishop of Canterbury, at Lambeth, and passing from thence over London Bridge to the Tower, he there made twelve knights bannerets, and created three peerages (but only one new peer), in view of the approaching ceremony. His uncle Jasper, Earl of Pembroke, was created Duke of Bedford; his stepfather, Lord Stanley, was made Earl of Derby; and Sir Edward Courtenay, Earl of Devon. This very sparing distribution of honours, however, was to be augmented a little later. On the day of his coronation—thinking well of

the dangers that might beset him in the future, but
veiling his purpose as if he only meant to add dignity
to the Crown—he instituted a bodyguard of fifty men,
archers and others, continually to attend him.   He had
seen the value of this in France, where such a body of
personal attendants had been instituted by Louis XI.
some years before ; and though the thing was new in
England, and perhaps not altogether popular at first, it
clearly tended to exalt the throne, which had certainly
suffered in dignity to some extent by the familiarity of
Edward IV. and the attempt of Richard III. to dress up
his election with a semblance of popular support.   The
sovereign was now further removed from the populace,
and the yeomen of the guard fulfil to this day at least
one of the purposes for which they were originally
instituted.

Parliament met on the 7th of November, in obedience to
a writ of summons dated the 15th of September—issued,
that is to say, just twelve days after the king's arrival
in London.   Henry evidently was anxious that it should
meet at the earliest possible opportunity, not so much
to vote him money, which the revenues of the Crown
themselves supplied, as to make a settlement of the
Crown upon himself and to lay a basis for future tranquillity.   Warmly as he had been received, he had still
to make it manifest to all the world that he was not a
usurper, nor yet a mere conqueror reigning by right of
the sword.   The first business, therefore, was the confirmation of his title.   Yet the grounds of that title,
as we have seen, were a matter of some delicacy, and
Parliament very wisely passed them over in silence.
It was enough that they found the title itself good and

sufficient. The king himself, indeed, addressed the Commons with his own mouth, declaring that he had come to the Crown by just right of inheritance, and by the judgment of God in giving him the victory over his enemy in battle. But the words used in the Act were merely, "That the inheritance of the Crowns of England and France be, rest, remain and abide, in the person of our now Sovereign Lord, King Harry the Seventh, and in the heirs of his body." Whether this was a recognition of antecedent right, or a making of right for the first time, mattered little as regards its practical effect. The important thing to note was that the right was acknowledged to be in the king himself, without any reference to his prospective marriage. The marriage might strengthen him hereafter, but in law he was strong without it.

After the attainders passed by Richard III. against Henry's followers had been reversed, an Act of Attainder was passed against the usurper and those who had fought for him at Bosworth. But how could fighting for Richard be treason when Henry was not yet king? Only by a legal fiction, which Parliament was subservient enough to enact. Henry's reign was made to begin on the 21st of August, the day before the battle of Bosworth. On that day the rebels—that is to say. Richard III. and his followers—mustered at Leicester, and moving on towards Bosworth next day, gave battle to Henry, their lawful king. So the matter was set forth in the Act; and it was needless, of course, for the proscribed party to protest against a misreading of history expressly aimed at them.

We are happy to learn, however, from one of the

very few writers of the period—a monk writing within
the seclusion of Croyland Abbey in Lincolnshire—that
few as the persons affected by it were, this arbitrary
enactment did not pass without considerable question
There were, in fact, some who distinctly censured its
injustice, and the monk himself, while recording the fact
that it encountered this criticism, cannot forbear adding
a reflection of his own as to the alarm which it inspired.
"O God!" he exclaims, "what security are our kings
to have henceforth that in the day of battle they may
not be deserted by their subjects, who, acting on the
awful summons of a king, may on the decline of that
king's party, as is frequently the case, be bereft of life
and fortune and all their inheritance?" The actual
victims, however, were doubtless, for the most part, men
for whom little sympathy was felt, and it was probably
the king's purpose at the outset to inspire as much terror
as possible through the Statute-book, that men might
feel how much they owed to the royal clemency. For a
general pardon soon afterwards gave assurance to all
others who had been in arms against the king provided
that they submitted and swore fealty within forty days ;
on which a great number at once came out of sanctuary.

We are told by Bacon that the king, enriched by
many valuable confiscations, thought it advisable not to
press for a money grant in this Parliament. As a matter
of fact, however, the grant of tunnage and poundage,
usually passed at the commencement of a reign, was voted
at this time ; and an Act of Resumption put him in possession of all the lands which had belonged to Henry
VI. on the 2d of October 1455, invalidating all subse-
quent grants by which any of them had been given away.

Henry was careful of money matters from the first, and some of the laws passed in this Parliament, while devised in the supposed interest of English trade, to secure it from competition by foreigners, were also calculated to enrich his treasury with forfeitures.

Another Act passed in this Parliament, affecting the rights of the Crown, deserves more attention than it has hitherto received. The abuses of purveyance had been a fertile source of complaint for centuries; and though by various statutes, from the days of Edward III., some security had been given for the payment of a reasonable price for commodities taken for the use of the royal household, the grievance still remained. On this subject the Commons made their "humble supplication" to the king, without apparently specifying any particular form of remedy; and the king, by the advice of his Council, drew up a scheme for the assignment of various portions of the revenue which actually belonged to him, amounting in all to £14,000, to the satisfaction of these claims, so that the expenses of his household should be fully provided for and all excuse for extortion taken away. The amount was charged in various definite sums on the Receivers-general of the duchies of Lancaster and Cornwall, and of the forfeited lands of Warwick, the King-maker, and others; on the Clerk of the Hanaper, the Warden of the Mint, the Chief Butler of England, the customs' dues at London and other ports, and the different farmers of Crown lands up and down the country. A clause was added, that if by any mistake payment could not be made of the particular sum charged on any particular officer, the Treasurer of England was to make assignment of the sum which was deficient upon some other of the royal revenues, and to make this a prior claim to every other. The scheme in all its details was submitted to Parliament, and approved by both Houses; but from the form of the enactment we may judge that it emanated from the king himself.

On the 19th of November an oath was proposed in the House of Lords which, it was hoped, would tend to suppress disorders in the country. A man was to swear not to receive or shelter any known felon, and not to retain any man by indenture or oath, or give liveries contrary to the law, impede the execution of the king's writs, encourage the practices called maintenance and embracery—that is to say, bring undue influence to bear in any form on a court of justice—or give any assent to riots or unlawful assemblies. Before this oath was taken by the Lords themselves it was administered to a number of knights and esquires, both of the king's household and of the House of Commons, who were expressly summoned to receive it in the Parliament chamber. It was then recited once more in the king's own presence, and all the lords, spiritual and temporal, swore to observe it, each of the former laying his right hand upon his breast and each of the latter laying it upon the Gospels.

And now Parliament, having done so much for the public tranquillity, urged the king himself to complete the work. On the 10th of December the Speaker, Thomas Lovell, brought up a request of the Commons and laid it before Henry, who was present in person in the House of Lords, that seeing they had settled the Crown on him and the heirs of his body, his Majesty would

deign to marry the Lady Elizabeth, daughter of Edward
the Fourth.   On this all the Lords rose from their seats,
and standing before the throne with their heads bowed,
repeated the same request.   The scene of course had
been arranged, and it suited Henry's purpose exactly
that he should be solemnly entreated by the most august
assembly in his kingdom to do what was really necessary
for the security of his own position, even if he had not
been bound to do it at any rate by the pledges given
in Britanny.   He replied with his own mouth that he
was willing to satisfy their desire ; after which Bishop
Alcock, as Chancellor, prorogued Parliament to the 23d
of January.

On his departure from France Henry had inflicted a
most appropriate punishment on the Marquis of Dorset
for his perfidious attempt to steal away from him at
Paris.   He left him and Sir John Bourchier in the French
king's hands as pledges for repayment of the money
advanced in aid of his expedition to England.   But now
that Parliament was prorogued, he sent at once to redeem
the hostages, and at the same time despatched messengers to Flanders for Morton, Bishop of Ely, to whose
warnings from a distance he was already so much indebted, that he might take, as he did from that time, a
leading place at his Council board.

It was certainly owing to Morton's diplomacy more
than to that of any other statesman of the day that
Henry was now in possession of the throne ; and it was
only natural that he should receive, as he did, the
highest honours that Henry could bestow.   Next year,
on the death of Cardinal Bourchier, he promoted him to
the see of Canterbury; in 1487 he made him Lord

Chancellor, and some years later, after many and urgent
solicitations, he prevailed on the Pope to make him
a cardinal. Yet it is difficult to say what kind of influence he exerted on Henry's policy as king, and one
might almost judge, from the scanty notices in State
papers, as well as from some casual expressions recorded
in his conversations with Buckingham, that in spite of
great natural astuteness he was only a politician by
necessity and duty, considering the service of the Church
as a higher object. We know that in the days of his
prosperity he was a magnificent builder, and one who
loved to encourage talent of every kind. Even as
Bishop of Ely he did a still greater work in draining the
fens of his marshy diocese and cutting a navigable canal
right through it to the sea. We know also that he was
the inventor of a notable argument for stimulating the
liberality of subjects towards their sovereign. At the
Council board, however, it is hinted that he opposed the
severity of some of Henry's measures. But we know
little of what he actually did, though we may rest assured, from the high respect in which he was held by
Sir Thomas More, that his counsels were no less honest
than far-sighted.

The leading members of Henry's Council at this time,
besides Morton, were Richard Fox and Reginald Bray.
The former was, like Morton himself, an ecclesiastic,
whom in the course of his reign he promoted to the
bishoprics of Exeter, Bath, Durham, and Winchester
successively. It was a great advantage to employ churchmen in the service of the State, as they could be rewarded
with bishoprics without putting the king to any expense;
and it was among churchmen more than among any

other class—far more, certainly, than among the hereditary councillors of the Crown—that Henry discovered
the tact and shrewdness needful to assist him in difficult
negotiations.   Besides the bishoprics just mentioned,
Henry conferred upon Fox the office of Lord Privy Seal
and employed him in various embassies.   Reginald Bray,
who is described by a nearly contemporary writer as
"a very father of his country, a sage and a grave person,
and a fervent lover of justice," was made a Knight of
the Garter, and unquestionably had very great influence
over the king; insomuch that, whenever taxation was
felt to be oppressive in the earlier part of the reign, the
people were apt to lay the blame upon him and Cardinal
Morton,—the fact, however, being that Morton and Bray
were precisely the two members of the king's Council
who dared most freely to remonstrate with Henry on
any act of injustice, and that it was greatly owing to
them that his government was not much more arbitrary.

Besides these it was only natural that the king should
be influenced to some extent by his uncle, Jasper, Duke
of Bedford, and also by the Earl of Oxford, who had
fought and suffered long years of imprisonment for the
cause of the House of Lancaster; by the Earl of Derby
and his son, Lord Strange, whose head had stood in so
much peril just before Bosworth field; and by Sir
William Stanley, whom he made his chamberlain.   There
were also other friends in adversity, such as Giles Daubeney, whom early next year he created Lord Daubeney;
John, Lord Dynham, whom he made Lord High Treasurer;
Sir Robert Willoughby, the steward of his household,
whom a year or two later he ennobled as Lord Willoughby
de Broke; Sir Richard Guildford, Sir John Cheyney,

Sir Richard Edgecombe, Sir Thomas Lovell, Sir Edward Poynings, and various others, who for their past fidelity and usefulness were admitted to his Council.

The long-delayed marriage with Elizabeth of York at length took place upon the 18th of January 1486. Henry had apparently forborne even to apply to Rome for a dispensation (for he and Elizabeth were within the prohibited degrees) until his title had been confirmed by Parliament. But, to satisfy public impatience, he did not wait for the arrival of the brief, having obtained a sufficient dispensation meanwhile from the Bishop of Imola, whom Innocent VIII. had despatched to England as legate, and the Pope soon afterwards issued two different bulls, not only confirming what had been done in the matter of the marriage, but also excommunicating every one who should rebel against Henry as king.

That Henry was "no very indulgent husband," his aversion to the House of York being manifest even in his chamber and his bed, rests only on the testimony of Lord Bacon, and seems to be, in the latter clause at least, rather an over-statement. The marriage was doubtless one of policy, and it was delayed, as we have seen, out of politic considerations also; it appears, moreover, to be a fact that the queen's influence over Henry was inferior to that of his mother; but there is no evidence of domestic tyranny or conjugal disagreements. On the contrary, we have positive testimony as to the wife's devotion, and even, in their later married life, as to the warm sympathy of both with each other on a domestic bereavement. But doubtless Henry was not uxorious, and it was not many weeks after his marriage that he set out on a progress through his kingdom, in which, with a wisdom fully justified by events, he left his queen behind him.

The north country, and especially Yorkshire, had been most devoted to Richard III., and Henry determined to go thither in person. He left London either in the beginning or middle of March, and rode by Waltham, Cambridge, Huntingdon, and Stamford to Lincoln, where he kept Easter, washing the feet of twenty-nine poor men on Maunday-Thursday, as he was twenty-nine years old. He then moved on to Nottingham, avoiding Newark, where a pestilence prevailed; then by Doncaster and Pomfret to York. His progress, however, was not unattended by warnings of coming danger; for at Lincoln he heard that Lord Lovell, and Humphrey and Thomas Stafford, adherents of Richard III., who had taken sanctuary at Colchester, had left their asylum and gone no one knew whither. At Nottingham he was informed of a rising in Yorkshire about Ripon and Middleham, but he seems to have thought little of it at first, and summoned a number of men from Lincolnshire to come to him, unarmed, believing that the display alone would have a good effect. At Pomfret, however, and between that and York, he was joined by a great body of nobility, gentry, and yeomen, hastily armed; and the insurgents, hearing of so strong a muster, speedily dispersed. At York he was received with great enthusiasm and gorgeous pageants, men, women, and children crying out, "King Henry! King Henry! Our Lord preserve that sweet and well-savoured face!" Yet the enemy was even then still pursuing his designs, and nearly succeeded in taking him by stratagem in York itself while he was celebrating the feast of St. George. The Earl of Northumberland.

however, defeated the attempt, and caused several of those engaged in it to be hanged.

The plan seems to have been that Lovell should capture York and the Staffords at the same time take possession of Worcester. Neither attempt was successful. Lovell, deserted by his followers, fled in the night to Lancashire, and the Staffords took refuge at Culham near Abingdon. But the privileges of sanctuary could not be extended to men whose crime was treason. They were taken, and Humphrey Stafford was hanged at Tyburn; but Thomas, the younger, was pardoned, as having been misled by his elder brother. The king passed on from York to Worcester, where the bishop, Alcock, preached before him on Whitsunday in the cathedral, and in the end of the sermon declared the Pope's bulls in confirmation of his marriage and of his right to the throne. From thence he went to Hereford, Gloucester, and Bristol, meeting with a very good reception at each of these places, although at Gloucester there was no pageant such as greeted him in every other town. At Bristol he made careful inquiry of the mayor and burgesses as to the causes of the town's poverty, and being told it was due to the great loss of ships and merchandise they had sustained during the preceding five years, he encouraged them to build new ships, promising that he would find means to assist their enterprise. He thus won the hearts of the Bristol merchants, the mayor declaring that they had not received such words of comfort from any king for a hundred years. And we know that they were not vain words; for later in the reign the king again showed a very marked interest in the prosperity of Bristol by the encouragement he gave

to Cabot's enterprise when he discovered Newfoundland.
Not forgetful himself from the very beginning of his
reign of matters which tended to the profit of the Crown,
no king could have been more careful to ascertain and
estimate the resources of his kingdom.

The king returned to London in June, ending his
progress by water from his palace of Sheen to Westminster. He was met and welcomed by the Lord Mayor
and citizens at Putney, who accompanied him down the
river in a multitude of barges. After a brief interval he
again went westward to hunt, and conducted his queen
to Winchester, where on the 20th of September, only
eight months after their marriage, she gave birth to a
son. The child, however, was fair and healthy to look
at, and his birth was hailed with delight by all who
wished for an end of civil dissension. He was christened
Arthur; and all the poets of the age endeavoured to
assure the world that the glories of the legendary king
of that name would be revived in a coming reign.

There remained yet one thing to be done for the
satisfaction of the kingdom—the queen's coronation, but
it had still to be deferred for some time.

CHAPTER IV

REBELLION OF LAMBERT SIMNEL

MODERN research has added nothing to the slender
information given by early writers with regard to that
"strange accident of State," the rebellion which took place
in the second year of Henry's reign in favour of Lambert
Simnel. But the circumstances out of which it arose are
clear enough. The king was still "green in his estate."
A number of the Yorkist party were still dissatisfied.
So much mystery surrounded the fate of the sons of
Edward IV. that idle rumours prevailed that one, if
not both of them, were still alive. The imprisonment
of Warwick in the Tower aroused suspicions that the
king would put him to death, and rumours were even
spread that he had been actually made away with. It
was under these circumstances that Richard Simon, a
priest of Oxford, stirred perhaps by some restless spirits
behind the scenes, inspired an adventurous boy named
Lambert Simnel, whose education doubtless had been
entrusted to him by his parents, with the idea of per-
sonating a young prince of the House of York. The lad
was only ten years of age, the son of one Thomas Simnel,
described afterwards in an Act of Parliament as "late of
Oxford, joiner," but in another document as an organ-

maker; while the blind poet, Bernard André, who lived
at the time, was not sure whether the youth claimed a
baker or a shoemaker for his father.   His origin, therefore, was obscure enough, but he was a bright lad and
an apt scholar.   He was first encouraged to personate
Richard, Duke of York, the younger of the two princes
murdered in the Tower; but perhaps owing to the
rumour that Warwick had died in prison, it was thought
that he could as safely fit himself with the character of
the latter personage.   And to prevent immediate detec-
tion Simon carried his pupil over to Ireland, where he
was declared to be the Earl of Warwick, son of the
Duke of Clarence, newly escaped from the Tower.

   The devotion of the Irish people to the House of
York, and their characteristic readiness to acquiesce in
impostures without too much inquiry, at once secured
for him an enthusiastic reception.   It has been supposed
that Henry neglected Ireland at the beginning of his
reign because he failed to remove the Earl of Kildare,
who had been Lord Deputy in the reigns of Edward IV.
and Richard III.   But evidence exists which shows
pretty clearly that he only forbore from policy to attempt
what was beyond his strength; for he sent over to
Ireland a messenger named John Estrete expressly to
invite the earl over to England to confer with him as to
the best means of bringing the country completely under
English rule; and as this was in reply to a request of
the earl himself to be made Deputy for a term of nine
or ten years, the king, without committing himself in
any way, gave every indication that he was well disposed
to consent, but wished, for one thing, to see whether the
revenues of Ireland could be made to bear the charge of

£1000 a year for the Deputy's salary, or whether that would have to be provided otherwise.

It is not clear, however, that this message reached the earl before Simnel's landing in Ireland. If it did we must suppose that it did not entirely satisfy him. For Kildare took counsel with the nobles and others upon the young man's pretensions, and it was unanimously agreed to support them. The supposed son of Clarence was lodged in Dublin Castle with great honour, proclaimed King of England by the name of Edward VI., and presently (24th May) crowned in Christ Church Cathedral, Dublin, amid the universal enthusiasm of the populace. Not a sword was drawn in Henry's favour. Bishops, nobles, judges, and high officers of State, all with one consent came to offer their allegiance to the pretender.

Nor was this all; for Ireland was but the scene chosen for the development of a widespread conspiracy, the first beginnings of which had not wholly escaped the king's notice. As early as February, just after Candlemas Day, the king had held a Great Council at Sheen, the chief result of which was a very mysterious decision taken about the queen-dowager. That Elizabeth Woodville, when her daughter was actually Queen of England, could have knowingly joined an intrigue to dethrone her husband is hardly credible in itself, and there is no reason to think it true. But she was a most unsteady woman, and her indiscretions may have been such as to serve the enemy's purpose almost as well as any active support she could have given them. Whatever may have been the case, the king thought fit, on due consideration, to deprive her of her jointure lands, which he had only a

year before restored to her, leaving her to find a retreat
in the Abbey of Bermondsey, where she had a right to
claim apartments as King Edward's widow, with a
pension of 400 marks, which the king soon after augmented to £400.   In that seclusion, from which apparently she only emerged on some special occasions, she
passed the few remaining years of her life, a miserable
and disappointed woman.   Her jointure lands were
given by Henry to the queen, her daughter.

Another result of the Council just referred to was
seen in the flight of one of the noblemen who had taken
part in it almost immediately afterwards.   This was
John de la Pole, Earl of Lincoln, who, being the eldest
son of the Duke of Suffolk by Elizabeth, sister of Edward
IV., had been named as successor to the kingdom by
Richard III. not long before Henry's invasion.   That he
should have been disappointed at Henry's success was
of course only natural, and it would seem that the pro-
ceedings at the Council convinced him that he was in
danger of being arrested as an intriguer.   He escaped
beyond sea and joined Lord Lovell in Flanders, where
he reported that Warwick was in Ireland and that he
himself had been privy to his escape, having conferred
with him at Sheen just before he left England.   This
was an excellent foundation for a plot.   In Flanders
all disaffected Yorkists were sure of sympathy from
Margaret, Duchess of Burgundy, widow of Charles the
Bold, who, being a sister of Edward IV. and also of the
Earl of Lincoln's mother, was bent upon the restoration
of the House of York, and did everything in her power
to encourage intrigues against Henry.   And it really
seemed that this enterprise, begun through the instru-

mentality of an impostor, required only a little judicious
aid to enable Lincoln to turn Henry off the throne.

Henry meanwhile met the danger first by ordering
Warwick to be taken from the Tower one Sunday and
conducted through the streets in sight of all the people
to St. Paul's ; and secondly, by issuing a general.pardon
for all offences, including treason against himself, on the
submission of the offenders.   He at the same time caused
the coasts to be well watched, not only to prevent further
escapes, but to guard against invasion, which was especially apprehended on the eastern coast.   For this reason
orders were given on the 7th of April to set the beacons in
order throughout Norfolk, Suffolk, and Essex ; and to
confirm the loyalty of those counties, the king himself
determined to go a progress through them.   So having
appointed two generals—his uncle Jasper, Duke of Bedford, and the Earl of Oxford—in case of any invasion
either from Ireland or from Flanders, he left London
in the middle of March and passed through Essex and
Suffolk into Norfolk.   At Bury St. Edmunds he was informed that the Marquis of Dorset—alarmed, no doubt,
at what had befallen his mother, the queen-dowager—
was coming to his presence to explain his conduct when
in France, and deprecate further suspicion ; but considering the uncertainties of the time, the king thought it
best to send the Earl of Oxford to apprehend him and
put him in the Tower, so as "to try his truth and prove
his patience."   For Henry considered that if he were
really loyal, as he actually proved, he would willingly
endure so slight an indignity for the sake of his prince,
while if he were otherwise it would prevent his doing
mischief.   Henry kept his Easter at Norwich, and on

Easter Monday (16th April) rode from thence to the famous shrine of Walsingham.

After paying his devotions there he turned westward towards the centre of the kingdom. He reached Coventry in less than a week, in time to keep the feast of St. George there, which was done with very special solemnity. Morton, who was now Archbishop of Canterbury, with five other bishops and a host of clergy, solemnly read in the cathedral the Pope's bulls declaring the king's right to the Crown, and that of the queen which was joined to his by marriage; whereupon they "cursed with book, bell, and candle" all who should in any way oppose those rights. Meanwhile the Earl of Lincoln and Lord Lovell, having obtained from the Duchess Margaret a band of 2000 veteran Germans, under the command of an experienced captain named Martin Swart, left the Low Countries, not to invade the east coast, but to join Simnel in Ireland, and landed in that country on the 5th of May. The king was still at Coventry when he heard the news, attended by most of the southern nobility, who had been summoned thither to assist him with their counsels. Most of these he at once sent back to their own districts to muster men, but some remained with him and sent orders to their people to be ready whenever summoned. Henry then rode to Kenilworth, and sent the Earl of Ormond to bring the queen and his mother to him there. News next came that the enemy ·had landed in Lancashire beside Furness Fells. A council of war was held at once, and Oxford, at his own request, was given the command of the royal forces.

Being thus compelled to face for a time a renewal of the civil war, Henry determined, for his part at least, to check as far as possible those enormities with which the country had been too familiar during such commotions; and by the advice of Morton, Fox, and others, he issued a very stringent proclamation against robbing churches, ravishing women, or even taking victuals without paying for them at the prices "assized by the clerk of the market," on pain of death. Nor was any man to venture to take a lodging for himself not assigned to him by the king's harbingers, on pain of imprisonment and further punishment at the king's discretion. The strictest discipline was enforced throughout the army; and the stocks and prisons of market towns in the rear of its march were filled with vagrants and offenders against the proclamation. Thus the king and his host advanced in good order to Nottingham, where they were joined by a very large force of the Earl of Derby's men under his son, Lord Strange, and from thence to Newark, near which town, at the village of Stoke, they met and defeated the invaders.

The enemy had done well to land in Lancashire, where they knew they could reckon on the aid of Sir Thomas Broughton and get a few English followers to join the ill-assorted crew of Irishmen and Germans who came to support Simnel's pretensions to the English throne. But they had greatly miscalculated in thinking that they would receive much support in England. They had naturally made for York, where the feeling in favour of the House of York had always been strong; but the country was desolate, and Lovell's previous abortive attempt in Yorkshire did not dispose the people in their favour. The hordes of half-savage Irishmen under Lord Thomas Fitzgerald (the Earl of Kildare's

brother), and even the well-trained mercenaries under
Martin Swart, were calculated rather to arouse disgust
and indignation. Meeting with no favourable reception
in Yorkshire, they came southwards and endeavoured to
surprise Newark; but were met, as we have just said,
at Stoke, and utterly routed with great slaughter. The
Irish, "after the manner of their country, almost naked,"
being only armed with darts and skeins, fought bravely,
but were cut down in masses. The rest of the host, too,
maintained the fight with the obstinacy of desperate
men. All the leaders—Lincoln, Lovell, Swart, and Sir
Thomas Broughton—either died on the field, or at least
were not seen alive after it; for as regards Lovell there
was a report that he had escaped and lived long after in
some secret place, and it is even supposed that his body
was discovered as late as the beginning of the eighteenth
century in a long-hidden chamber at Minster Lovel in
Oxfordshire. Simnel and his tutor, the priest, were
taken prisoners, and the former being a mere boy, the
king, with great policy, instead of putting him to death,
took him into his service as a menial of the royal kitchen.
As for the priest, he was placed in lifelong confinement.

Having thus gained the victory, the king went to
Lincoln, where he ordered thanksgivings to be made,
and then set forth on a progress into the north, causing
strict inquiry to be made as he went, by court-martial
or otherwise, as to the part taken by any of the inhabitants in befriending the rebels, or even expressing sympathy with them, as some had done by spreading false
rumours of the defeat of the royal forces. To check
such sympathy in future he imposed fines on those who
were but slightly implicated, while the more serious

offenders were put to death. He visited York, and
went as far as Newcastle, from which place he sent Fox,
Bishop of Exeter, and Sir Richard Edgecombe in embassy to James III. of Scotland. The Scotch king, like
the English, was at this time peacefully disposed—more
so, it is believed, than most of his own subjects. A
three years' truce had already been concluded between
the two countries in the preceding year, and the English
ambassadors endeavoured to get it extended with a view
to a lasting peace, which was to be cemented by three
marriages : the first between the Scotch king's second
son, James, Marquis of Ormond, and Katharine, the third
daughter of Edward IV. ; the second between the Scotch
king himself and the English queen-dowager, Elizabeth
Woodville—a thing apparently designed on Henry's part
to remove the cloud which rested on his mother-in-law,
without remitting the penalty she had incurred by her
behaviour ; and the third between the Duke of Rothesay,
heir-apparent to the Scottish throne, and some other one
of Edward IV.'s daughters, the question which of them
it was to be being left for further consideration. The
three matches were agreed to in this form ; but the
negotiators could only agree to a two months' extension
of the truce. All efforts to bring about a permanent
peace were for the present ineffectual ; and any possibility of the renewal of the three marriage projects was
terminated in the following summer by the revolt of the
Scottish nobles and the death of James III.

In the autumn Henry returned southward for the
long-deferred coronation of his queen, and also to meet
his second Parliament. On his way he received at
Leicester certain ambassadors from Charles VIII., sent

chiefly to explain the French king's attack on the duchy of Britanny—a thing to which it was rightly suspected that English feeling would be sensitive. He arrived in London on the 3d of November, and was received with triumph like a conqueror. Parliament met on the 9th, and proceeded at once to attaint the leaders of the late rebellion and to pass various severe measures for the punishment of crimes and misdemeanours, one of which was what may almost be considered the institution of the afterwards too notorious Court of Star Chamber. The popular name of this court was derived from the room in which the Privy Council were in the habit of meeting, especially when they met as a court of justice; and the Act simply invested certain members of the Council with a criminal jurisdiction, highly necessary at this time, to restrain a host of abuses which had grown out of the too great power of the nobles. Livery and maintenance especially were the two great evils which, besides lending themselves too readily to a renewal of civil war, placed sheriffs, juries, and the whole administration of justice throughout the country under influences which utterly destroyed their independence. And as the court was chiefly intended to curb the power of the great, care was taken to strengthen its judicial authority by joining with the lords and privy councillors the two chief justices, or two other judges in their place. Parliament also granted a subsidy for the defence of the kingdom.

The queen's coronation took place on Sunday, the 25th of November, and was solemnised with a splendour that atoned for previous tardiness. The processions and festivities connected with it began two days before the

coronation day itself, and continued two days after.
It was, moreover, intimated that they would have been
even further prolonged but for "the great business of
the Parliament." It was perhaps important that the
measures for restraining the power of the lords, if not
already passed, should be passed before Christmas, when
the members of either House would naturally expect to
be allowed to return, each to his own part of the
country. But the really "great business" of this Parliament more probably had reference to the French king's
aggression upon Britanny, of which we shall speak more
at length in the next chapter; for it was no doubt in
view of this and of possible future hostilities that a
subsidy of two tenths and fifteenths was voted, besides
a pretty considerable tax upon artisans (six and eight-
pence to be paid by each native artificer, and higher rates
upon aliens), which imposts appear to have met with
little or no opposition.

Domestic peace was now tolerably secure; but it
remained a question how to deal with Ireland—a country
which had lent itself so readily to the designs of English
faction and foreign intrigue. It was out of the question
to punish a rebellion in which practically the whole
country was implicated; and apparently for some
months the king was content to allow the ridiculous
failure of the expedition in Simnel's favour to impress
its own moral upon the Irish people. At last, in the
middle of the following year, Sir Richard Edgecombe
was sent over to Ireland with a commission to receive
the fealty of all who were willing to acknowledge King
Henry, and to grant ample pardons for the past.

A sturdy Cornishman, well used to adventure in the

preceding . reign, when it is said he had narrowly
escaped with his life by flinging his bonnet in the water
and making his pursuers think·that he was drowned,
Sir Richard must have been prepared for a dangerous
enterprise. He sailed from Mount's Bay in Cornwall
on the 23d of June 1488, and, after some time lost in the
pursuit of pirates, reached Kinsale on the 27th. Here
he took the allegiance of Lord Thomas of Barry, and
landing at the request of Lord Courcy, who did fealty
for the barony of Kinsale, had the keys of the town
delivered to him. He then sailed to Waterford, a town
which had always preserved its loyalty (it was there, or
in neighbouring harbours, that English expeditions had
always landed), and was conducted by the mayor over
the walls and fortifications. The mayor also informed
him of the disposition of the people, especially of the
great men, and besought his protection against their
old enemy, the Earl of Kildare, for whom they knew he
had a pardon from the king. Sir Richard assured him
that the city's interests would be protected, and sailing
northward, after a rough passage anchored off Lambay
Island, and sent a messenger to Dublin to inquire the
disposition of the country. Word was brought back to
him that the Earl of Kildare had gone on pilgrimage for
a few days, on which Sir Richard landed at Malahide,
and was conducted up to Dublin by the Bishop of Meath,
a prelate who had taken an active part in Simnel's coronation but was now anxious to show his loyalty. Sir
Richard took up his quarters in the Black Friars, where
he awaited the arrival of Kildare, and meanwhile received the submission of the Archbishop of Dublin and
Rowland Fitzeustace, the Treasurer of Ireland, two other

of Simnel's late adherents.   At length Kildare arrived
with 200 horse at St. Thomas's Court, just outside the
walls of Dublin, where Sir Richard delivered to him a
message from the king.   He desired time to consult
about it with the lords of the Irish Council, who were
not then with him, and retired to his Castle of Maynooth.

Next day, which was a Sunday, the 13th of July, Sir
Richard got the Bishop of Meath to publish at Christ
Church Cathedral the Pope's bull of excommunication,
and the readiness with which absolution might be obtained with the king's free pardon on submission.   On
the Monday, at the earl's special entreaty, he visited
him at Maynooth, and obtained from him a promise to
conform in future to the king's pleasure.   He failed,
however, to obtain from him any securities for good
behaviour, which Sir Richard continually insisted on,
both at Maynooth and afterwards again at Dublin.
Both the earl and other lords were liberal in promises
to be the king's true subjects; but, rather than give the
bonds required, said they would become Irish every
man.   At last, hearing a report of the death of the
King of Scots, which he feared might be the cause of
further trouble, Sir Richard was content to take their
oaths upon the sacrament as sufficient security for their
loyalty; and after many objections and attempts at
evasion they were ultimately sworn at St. Thomas's on
the 21st of July, and absolved from the papal curse.
Sir Richard then put a collar of the king's livery about
the Earl of Kildare's neck, which he wore publicly in
the city.

Sir Richard next visited Drogheda and Trim, and took
the homage of both those towns; then returning to

Dublin, took the fealties of a number of other gentlemen.
He refused, however, notwithstanding the urgent solicitations of Kildare, to take the fealties of Justice Plunket
and the Prior of Kilmainham, two of the chief promoters of Simnel's rebellion, who, in expectation of the
king's pardon, thought little of their past offences, till at
last, after much intercession, he admitted Plunket to
favour.   But he put Dublin Castle in the keeping of a
loyal subject, whom the Prior of Kilmainham had for
two years and more kept out of the office of constable,
and embarked at Dalkey on the 30th of July on his
return to England.

He had at least got the chief men in Ireland to
recognise once more the king's authority and the duty
of obedience.   But the government of the country had
to be left in the hands of those who had most actively
promoted rebellion, and it scarcely required a prophet
to foresee that in any future trouble Ireland would again
take a leading part.

CHAPTER V

WE have said that on his way southward to London, in the autumn of 1487, Henry received an embassy from Charles VIII. of France, sent chiefly to explain his attack on the duchy of Britanny. The independence of that duchy had long been threatened. It was the last of the feudal lordships subject to the French Crown which retained its old independence, and Charles and his Council were fully bent on completing the policy of Louis XI. by annexing it. The feeble condition of the duke favoured the design, and a fair pretext for interference was found in the asylum given by him to Louis, Duke of Orleans, heir-presumptive to the French throne, who, having laid claim to the government during Charles's minority, had taken up arms against the regent, Madame de Beaujeu, and attempted to make Britanny a basis of operations against France. The duke also allied himself with Maximilian, King of the Romans, who aspired to marry Anne, the heiress of the duchy. But Maximilian was easily held in check by the Estates of Flanders, which refused him supplies, so that Britanny had no efficient protector. And apart from Henry's own personal obligations to the duke, there was a strong

feeling in England against allowing such an important
province to be added to the French Crown. For it was
clear that if France commanded all the harbours on the
south side of the Channel, the danger to England in any
future disputes might be very considerable ; and Englishmen, who had been accustomed to look upon France
almost as if it was their rightful property—as a country
to be invaded and ravaged at pleasure whenever their
king could make up his mind to an expedition against
it—could not look without some dismay at the consolida-
tion of the power of a great rival, and their own seeming
exclusion from a happy hunting-ground for evermore.

The French had not only entered Britanny, but had
besieged the duke in Nantes.   They had been compelled,
however, to raise the siege shortly before they sent their
embassy to England ; and this perhaps served to quiet
apprehensions to some extent.   Henry too, for his part,
did not wish to break with France.   As he was personally indebted to the French king as well as to the duke,
he sought rather to mediate, and in the spring of 1488
he sent ambassadors to both parties commissioned to use
their utmost efforts to bring them to accord.   He could
not, however, have been blind to the fact that it would
suit the interests of France very well to encourage
negotiation while pressing on her preparations for further
action ; and it is clear that the necessity of armed interference suggested itself strongly to some of his Council.
But while the Council were deliberating, Lord Woodville, Governor of the Isle of Wight (a brother of the
queen-dowager and uncle to Henry's own queen),
crossed, against positive orders from the king, with a
body of men to Britanny, and put himself at the duke's

commands. This naturally caused great exasperation in France, where it is said even the English ambassadors were hardly safe from outrage. But Henry disowned the act, and the French Court was only too glad to accept his apology and keep up negotiations, especially when events soon gave them a great advantage which completely neutralised the unrecognised aid that Britanny had obtained from England. On the 14th of July Henry signed at Windsor a renewal of the truce with France, which would naturally have expired on the 17th of January following (*i.e.* 1489), to the 17th of January 1490. How far he had succeeded in persuading himself that Britanny was safe in the meanwhile it is difficult to say. The truce itself made no stipulation about the duchy, and Henry was probably unwilling to interfere in its behalf single-handed, or with no other ally than Maximilian, King of the Romans, whose resources were not equal to his valour. He appears, however, to have been waiting for some definite offer from Ferdinand of Spain, who was very anxious, for his own purposes, to drag him into a war with the French on any pretext whatever. But while the powers interested in checkmating France were each looking to the other to see who would begin, France had dealt a decisive blow at Britanny. The power of the duchy was in fact completely crippled, just a fortnight after the truce was signed at Windsor, by the disastrous battle of St. Aubin, fought on the 28th of July. The Duke of Orleans was taken prisoner, with a number of other eminent captains besides, and not less than 6000 men are said to have been slain, among whom were included Lord Woodville and nearly the whole of his English followers. The loss of Dinan and St. Malo

immediately followed, and though Rennes still refused to
surrender, the Duke of Britanny was obliged to make
peace on the 21st of August. He died within three
weeks afterwards.

England was now seriously alarmed. The question
remained whether the duchy could even yet be saved
from complete absorption ; but the right of interference
seemed barred by the truce. English blood, however,
had been actually shed in Britanny, and while there
was a natural desire in England to avenge defeat, there
was in France a no less natural feeling of resentment at
the interference that had already taken place. Peace was
evidently difficult to preserve, but Henry took means to
tide matters over till he was sure of his ground. The
Duke of Britanny had left no son, but only two daughters,
of whom the elder, Anne, was now duchess and not
quite twelve years old. Maximilian, as we have already
said, was a suitor for her hand ; but Henry, seeing little
help to be looked for from him, proposed a marriage
between her and the young Duke of Buckingham, son of
the duke beheaded by Richard III., and sent an ambassador to Britanny upon the business. He also commissioned
the Spanish ambassador to write about it to Ferdinand
and Isabella, as he was desirous to act in concert with
Spain. The Spanish sovereigns replied that they wished
to favour it for Henry's sake, but suggested reasons
against it which Henry himself no doubt foresaw. There
was a danger of alienating not only Maximilian but
also the Sieur d'Albret, who was another suitor for
the duchess's hand, and the cause of Britanny would
be weakened rather than strengthened. In deference
to the Spanish sovereigns, Henry withdrew his proposal ;

which, however, had practically served its purpose in
showing the Duchess Anne that she had still a prospect
of powerful support; for its very withdrawal made it
evident that Spain as well as England was anxious that
the duchy should not be lost.   Indeed, some time after
persuading him to withdraw the suit of the Duke of
Buckingham, Ferdinand obtained the King of England's
consent to a proposal that his own son, Don Juan, the
Infant of Spain, should marry the duchess.   But the
project, as it turned out, was conceived a little too late.

Henry was preparing for war, but did not meditate
any act of aggression.   He had already tied his hands
by the truce with France, which he had no intention to
violate while it lasted.   But the duchess made a strong
appeal to him for defensive aid, and there was a fair
case for interference to that extent.   On the death of
the duke, Charles had sent her an embassy declaring
his intention to observe the treaty signed in August;
but as her feudal superior he claimed her wardship,
and told her she must forbear calling herself duchess
till the question of her right to the duchy had been
settled by competent judges.   Anne informed him in
reply that she would call the Estates of the duchy to
ratify the treaty, and meanwhile she invoked the help
of England to maintain her in her rights.   Henry called
a Great Council together at Westminster in November to
consider what was to be done.   Immediately afterwards,
that is to say, on the 11th of December, he despatched
embassies to Charles VIII., the Duchess Anne, Maximilian, Philip, Duke of Burgundy, Ferdinand and Isabella of Spain, and John II. of Portugal, all on the
same day.   What message he sent to each of these

princes we do not precisely know; but we know that
he had determined to secure the duchess, if possible,
against further aggression without violating his truce
with France; and he at once sent out commissions to
raise archers and muster men in defence of Britanny, for
which purpose Parliament in February following granted
him a liberal subsidy.

Meanwhile the French had re-entered the duchy and
summoned Guingamp to surrender. They took it on
the 18th of January 1489. But on the 10th of February
Henry's ambassadors concluded a treaty with the duchess
at Redon, which he confirmed on the 1st of April following. By this treaty, in consideration of an immediate
loan of 6000 armed men, to be used strictly for defensive
purposes till the feast of All Saints following, the duchess
engaged at any future time when it pleased Henry to
call upon her after his truce with France should have
expired in 1490, to aid him to recover Normandy and
any other of the old English possessions in France. This
loan of men, however, was not to be made without very
sufficient security for their expenses; for it was expressly
stipulated that a number of them, not to exceed 500,
were at once to be put in possession of certain towns and
castles, which were to be delivered to Henry in pawn.
The English soldiers, moreover, were to be sent back to
their native country at the expense of the duchess, and
the money in repayment of their expenses was to be
conveyed over sea at her risk and the repayment made
in England. Thus, if the resources of the duchy were
crippled by invasion, the English soldiers would remain
in command of the most important strongholds.

It was, however, comparatively an easy thing to

strengthen Britanny against external attack; the difficulty was to strengthen her against internal weakness.
The young duchess had been left under the guardian-
ship of Marshal de Rieux, with whom the English very
naturally entered into negotiations.   De Rieux unhappily
favoured the proposal of a marriage between her and
D'Albret, who, being a powerful lord of Gascony and
father to the King of Navarre, would undoubtedly have
been able to give her very efficient support.   Of course
it made no difference, from a mere political point of view,
that he was a widower who had been married seven
years before she was born; but the young lady herself
had no mind for such a union, and protested she would
sooner be a nun.   De Rieux, as well as D'Albret, was
thus alienated, and the duchess gave all her confidence
to Count Dunois and her Chancellor, Philip de Montauban.   De Rieux accused them of favouring the
interests of the French, and refused the duchess herself
admittance into Nantes unless she would enter privately,
leaving her friends in the suburbs.   She withdrew to
Rennes, where she was received with devoted loyalty,
and endeavoured to dissuade all her allies from having
anything to do with the marshal.

Meanwhile the French king, having received plain
warning from Henry of the steps he was taking to assist
the duchess, sent over to England Salazart, Archbishop
of Sens, who arrived there in March and sought a private
audience of the king; but Henry refused to see him
except in public.   On the subject of Britanny Henry
was willing to name commissioners to discuss matters;
but he gave the archbishop distinctly to understand that
in the opinion of Englishmen the French had no business

there. The archbishop soon found that his mission was practically useless, and returned tò his master at Chinon. About the time he reached the French Court the stipulated body of 6000 Englishmen landed in Britanny, led by Lord Willoughby de Broke, steward of the household, and Sir John Cheyney, master of the horse. On their landing, the French evacuated and burned Guingamp, but not without laying the inhabitants under tribute and taking hostages of them for the payment. The English immediately occupied the place.

In May Marshal de Rieux sent the Seigneur de Sourdeac to England to represent to the king that, if D'Albret were made master of Britanny by marrying the duchess, he could give the English effectual aid to recover Guienne, the loss of which six-and-thirty years before still rankled in the English breast. It is not likely that Henry was much influenced by such a prospect; but he continued to negotiate with De Rieux as Anne's proper guardian, much to the displeasure of Anne herself, or at all events of Dunois and Montauban, who caused her to send remonstrances to Henry against showing him any countenance. The duchess in fact demanded Henry's help to recover Nantes out of De Rieux's hands; for he was appointing and dismissing officers against her will and raising the revenues of the duchy to her prejudice. Henry sought in vain to promote a reconciliation between them. Meanwhile he did something to aid Britanny by active support of her ally Maximilian in Flanders.

Shortly after Easter he had received important embassies in return for those he had sent in December to Maximilian and to the King of Portugal. The former was then in urgent need of assistance. Son of the

penurious Emperor Frederic III., his high-sounding title,
King of the Romans, did little to make him powerful.
What influence he had in the affairs of Europe had been
owing to his marriage with his late wife, Mary, Duchess
of Burgundy, whose wealthy patrimony he now administered as far as the independent spirit of the Flemings
would allow him to have the rule.   The men of Ghent
and Bruges, however, acknowledged only the authority
of his son and heir, Philip, a lad at this time nearly
eleven years old, whom they had recognised as Duke of
Burgundy from the time of his mother's death, when he
was a mere infant.   They took possession of his person,
used him freely as a puppet, and ignored entirely the
authority of his father.   Maximilian endeavoured to
reduce them by force, but they appealed for aid to the
French king, who sent an army under Philip de Crève-
cœur, Sieur d'Esquerdes (or Lord Cordes, as the English
called him), to their support.   Maximilian then sought
to win over Bruges by conference with some of its
principal citizens.   But the result was that he allowed
himself to be lured into the town, where, after several of
his friends had been beheaded, he himself was called to
answer for having interfered with their liberties and
disregarded the treaty which they and the men of
Ghent had made with France.   By a gentle answer he
contrived to mitigate their resentment, and after swearing to pardon all offences, he was allowed to depart at
liberty, much to the discontent of the men of Ghent,
who would have delivered him prisoner into the hands
of the French.

The theory that the people have a right to rule, and
that the sovereign is a mere ornamental figurehead, was

in those days the exclusive property of the Flemings.
It certainly was not the received view in England for
more than a century after, and while Europe was ringing
with the indignity shown to an emperor's son in depriving him of his rights alike as father and as guardian of
their prince, the English people were more indignant
than others. Maximilian seems to have kept his oath,
but the Emperor Frederic made war on the rebellious
towns to avenge the affront. The Lord of Ravenstein,
however, who was a leading member of Maximilian's
Council and had taken the oath along with him—either
to keep faith with the Flemings, or, as it is said, won
over by France—deserted the cause of his master and
took Ypres and Sluys, which he fortified and victualled
against the power of Maximilian. The Sieur d'Esquerdes
sent 8000 Frenchmen into the Low Countries to besiege
Dixmude, and there was some danger of Calais being
completely surrounded by a circle of French garrisons.
Lord Morley was accordingly sent thither with a body
of 1000 men, who at first were reported to have come
only to strengthen the English pale. But one night,
joining with a picked company from the garrisons of
Calais, Guines, and Hammes, under the command of
Lord Daubeney, the Lieutenant of Calais, they secretly
entered Flanders, and, with a body of 600 Germans who
met them at Nieuport, came next morning through Dixmude upon the camp of the besiegers, which they soon
completely broke up. It was a splendid victory, the
spoils taken were magnificent, and the English were
naturally elated. They carried their wounded and
their booty to Nieuport, and drove out a body of Frenchmen from Ostend. But the safety of Calais was not

yet completely secured.   For the Sieur d'Esquerdes,
who was at Ypres burning to revenge defeat, laid siege
to Nieuport while there were few to defend it but the
wounded, Lord Daubeney having returned to Calais.
The wounded men, however, manned the walls, and
were animated to the fight even by the women of the
town till a body of fresh English archers arrived by sea
from Calais.   D'Esquerdes then found it necessary to
raise the siege, and giving up at last his ardent hope of
winning Calais, retreated southward to Hesdin.

This must have been very grateful news to Henry,
who had found little respite yet from anxiety from
the commencement of his reign.   Although the line of
policy he had pursued in the dispute between France
and Britanny was studiously just and moderate, and
although it failed to satisfy the more ardent among his
own subjects, it nevertheless was a cause of trouble
within the kingdom itself.   In accordance, no doubt,
with the determination of the Great Council in November,
Parliament had met in January, and in February had
granted the king a subsidy, as we have already seen.
Every man was to contribute "the tenth penny of his
goods," or rather, of the annual value of his lands, for
goods and chattels were to be assessed at the rate of
twentypence for every ten marks of their actual or
whole value.   The assessment was to be made before
Easter, and one-half the sum due was to be levied before
the 1st of May.   The object was to raise an army of
10,000 archers "against the ancient enemies of this
realm," as set forth in the Act; and the tax imposed
turned out to be inadequate after all.   But, however
willing men were to fight for Britanny, they were not

equally ready to supply the necessary funds; and north of the Humber the commissioners met with an amount of resistance that compelled them to complain to the Earl of Northumberland. The earl immediately informed the king, who on the 10th of April sent a commission to the Archbishop of York, the earl himself, the Abbot of St. Mary's, and a number of others, to search out the promoters of disturbances, and commit them at once to prison to await their trials. But matters had already gone too far to be so easily dealt with. A number of the earl's own tenants openly refused to obey the Act of Parliament, and the earl mustered a company to seize their persons. They, on the other hand, gathered their friends, and a regular battle took place between them and the earl's company, in which the earl himself and many of his servants were killed not far from Thirsk on the 28th of April.

The king was at Hertford, receiving the embassies already referred to, when this news reached him. He determined to stay there no longer than was necessary to give them a sufficient hearing on the important affairs on which they had come to him; and on the 22d of May he departed northwards to see to the peace of the country himself. The insurrection had been meanwhile prolonged under one Sir John Egremont, a man of Yorkist sympathies; for the old feeling towards the House of York was still strong in the north of England. But the rebels had no fighting power, and presently took to their heels. Sir John Egremont fled to the Lady Margaret of Burgundy; and the king, on his return from the north, established a Council for the better government of those parts, placing at the head of it Thomas Howard, Earl of

Surrey, a man on whose chivalrous sense of honour, though he had fought for Richard III. at Bosworth, Henry rightly judged that he could rely to keep the country in tranquillity.

Thus Calais was safe, and the north of England in a fair way to be pacified. Moreover, France was for the time checkmated and tired of war. For the efforts of England and Maximilian had been supplemented by those of Ferdinand of Spain, who about the same time made an attack on Roussillon. Charles, however, had by no means given up his designs on Britanny, and only sought by diplomacy to separate the allies. There could be no doubt which of them to begin with. Maximilian was not only weak in his resources but unstable in his policy. Seven years before, when Louis XI. began the game of intriguing with his rebellious subjects, he had been compelled by the treaty of Arras to sign away the inheritance of his own son Philip in the counties of Artois and Burgundy, and appoint them as a dower for his daughter Margaret, whom it was agreed that Charles, at that time dauphin, should marry when he came of age. To this treaty Charles now appealed, and addressing Maximilian as his father-in-law, expressed a desire for a settlement of all their differences. He found Maximilian no less amicably disposed than himself. Only a month after the battle of Dixmude, while a diet was held at Frankfort, which had been convoked by the Emperor Frederic with the view of getting support for his son from Germany, ambassadors arrived from the French king, between whom and Maximilian peace was effectually made on the 22d of July 1489. The details of the settlement were for the most part left to be arranged at

a personal interview between the two princes; but it
was a positive stipulation that the Duchess Anne should
be put in possession of all the strongholds held by her
father, provided she would bind herself to turn the
English out of Britanny.

The war in the duchy, however, was at that moment
going on as vigorously as ever. De Rieux was endeavouring to besiege Brest by land and sea, while the
English were blockading Concarneau. The French in
August poured fresh troops into the country, and sent a
fleet which broke up the siege of Brest. The English
also about the same time sent reinforcements, but apparently they could effect little, and in November the
duchess, pressed hard by Charles, thought it best to
accept the treaty of Frankfort. The peace was immediately proclaimed both in France and in the duchy.

This could scarcely have been agreeable news either
to England or to Spain. The treaty, however, was
utterly futile without their consent to it; for both
English and Spanish troops held important positions in
the country, and as neither De Rieux nor D'Albret could
easily acquiesce in a settlement which would have placed
them as rebels in the power of France, it was easy
enough with their aid to invalidate what had been done.
This Ferdinand at once set himself to do, and presuming
that Henry would see the matter in the same light,
gave immediate orders to his captains in Britanny to act
in closer unison with the English than they had done
hitherto. Henry, for his part, seems to have taken things
more calmly. His truce with France was just about to
expire. If it had been allowed to do so the gain to
Charles would, to say the least, have been extremely

doubtful, and his agreement with the duchess little better than waste paper, seeing that she was absolutely powerless to make the English quit her shores. The French king, therefore, twice sent over a solemn embassy, consisting of Francis, Lord of Luxemburg; Wallerand, Lord of Marigny; and the celebrated French historian and orator, Robert Gaguin, General of the Trinitarian Friars in France, to persuade Henry to acquiesce in the Frankfort settlement and make a firm peace, withdrawing his troops from Britanny. They had been in England in the autumn, when they were briefly dismissed and sent back. The second time they came about Christmas, and dined with the king on St. John's day, the 27th of December; but not all the eloquence of Gaguin could prevail on Henry to comply with their master's demands. Some slight extension of the truce they seem to have procured (although there is no distinct record of the fact), as negotiations were still kept up, and a return embassy sent to France after the date when it should have expired. But this proved for Henry's advantage, not for that of Charles; for in February 1490—little more than two months after her acceptance of the treaty of Frankfort — the Duchess Anne sent her Chancellor, Montauban, to England, commissioned virtually to tell the king that she threw herself entirely on his protection, and that she would never marry any one without his consent.

The French ambassadors were obliged to return again to their own country, having completely failed in the main object for which they were sent. Somewhat later, after still further efforts for peace had broken down, the oratorical Gaguin revenged himself for his repeated ineffectual missions in a bitter epigram against the English, to which a host of poetasters on Henry's side wrote replies. But in the meanwhile Henry sent, as already mentioned, a return embassy to France, not apparently with any great hope of peace, but to explain definitely to the French king and his Council on what terms he was prepared to treat with regard to the duchy of Britanny. On their way to the French Court they met at Calais a new messenger of peace proceeding to England, who could not but be listened to with defer- ence. Lionel Chieregato, Bishop of Concordia, papal nuncio, had been at the Court of France for about a year when he received orders to proceed to England in the Pope's name and endeavour to compose matters between the two kingdoms. The king gave him, by his own request, a public audience at London on the 29th of March, when he spoke earnestly of the necessity of peace among Christian princes in view of the advances of the Turk, who had not only within that generation made alarming conquests in Greece, Hungary, and the Crimea, but had even ravaged the coast of Italy and the States of the Church. The Pope, he said, was anxious that all European powers should lay aside their differences and combine against the common enemy. One great piece of good fortune encouraged him to believe that an effec- tual blow might now be struck for the deliverance of Christendom. The Turkish empire had been for some years divided against itself, and Zizim, the rebellious brother of Bajazet II., having sought alliance with the knights of Rhodes, had been delivered by them into the Pope's hands. The fact, indeed, was not quite so inter- esting to a sovereign in the west of Europe as it was to the Pope himself, and the disputes between England and France must be considered upon their own merits. But the general tenor of his address greatly pleased the king, who desired Archbishop Morton to reply to him. Afterwards he had conferences apart both with the king and with the Chancellor, and from his own report to the Pope we know precisely the attitude which Henry and his councillors then assumed.

That Henry himself, as a sovereign, was always peacefully inclined, is a fact not only admitted by all historians, but confirmed by all historical testimony. Indeed it was so manifestly against his interests to involve himself in needless wars, that it is simply inconceivable that he did not wish to avoid them by every means that would have satisfied the honour and the susceptibilities of the nation. But, disputes arising on this unhappy question of Britanny, it was impossible not to connect them with the old-standing, and it might seem antiquated, claims of the Kings of England to the realm of France. And when it is considered that the pretensions of the Kings of England to be Kings of France were not formally renounced even by a refugee King of England at Versailles two hundred years after this date, we need not wonder that the most peaceful of English kings felt it necessary to uphold them in the end of the fifteenth century. Indeed the assistance given to Henry himself when in exile by the French Government, by means of which he was enabled to attain the English Crown, only put him in a position soon after his accession to make a truce between the two countries, which had since been twice renewed; and if there was to be a permanent peace, some settlement must be

arrived at concerning the long-standing claim. On this
point, however, there was a pretty easy way out of the
difficulty. Edward IV. had invaded France, and then
agreed to waive his claim to the kingdom for a pension
of 50,000 crowns from Louis XI., which he was pleased
to call a tribute. If a permanent peace were talked
about, Henry was willing to compromise the matter in
the same fashion; but for the credit of the kingdom he
could not afford to take one shilling less than the amount
which had been so readily conceded by King Louis.

Chieregato, who had other pressing business committed to him by the Pope in France, and had promised
to return in May, soon found that it was hopeless to
negotiate at once anything like a permanent peace; but
after long and earnest consultations with Archbishop
Morton, the terms of a three years' truce were agreed to,
which it would seem that he had been authorised by the
French to propose, on the understanding that the matter
of Britanny should be the subject of a separate arrangement. On his return he drew up at Tours, in concert
with the English ambassadors there, a protocol for a
seven months' truce between France and Britanny; and
next month he repaired to a congress, which had been
arranged to take place between ambassadors of both
powers, at Boulogne and Calais, with a view to a final
settlement. The prospect really looked favourable on
all sides, except in the matter of Britanny; and here the
English at least had shown themselves perfectly reasonable. All that they required was repayment by the
Duchess Anne herself of the expense they had been
put to in assisting her; on receiving which they were
ready to evacuate the duchy even before the French

did the same. They did not object even to the French
king lending her the money to redeem the places they
held as securities. Meanwhile, however, a pacification
had been going on within the duchy itself, which unfortunately did not help the general settlement. For
through the mediation of England the Duchess Anne
was now reconciled to the Marshal de Rieux, who had
agreed no longer to press upon her the objectionable
marriage with D'Albret, and was now exerting himself
in her service as strenuously as he possibly could. The
result was that, under new advice, the duchess demanded
some alterations, which, however, in the end were conceded. But when all else had been arranged, the French
king sent away the ambassadors of Britanny at his
Court with an absolute refusal to restore the places occupied by his troops.

The truce of Britanny thus fell through ; and though
the sittings of the congress were continued from June to
August, nothing like a settlement could be arrived at.
Charles had insisted that the English should evacuate
Britanny before the castles taken by the French in the
duchy were restored ; after which he was willing to
submit his right to the duchy to a judicial investigation at Tournay. Now the English, as we have seen,
were quite willing to have withdrawn their forces even
before the French, and delivered the castles they held
into the hands of the duchess on receiving payment for
their expenses, and they did not object even to France
advancing the money ; but they would only deal with
the duchess herself. It does not appear, therefore, that
the obstacle to peace arose on the side of England.
Henry had done all that was reasonable, but distrusting

the result, he prepared to put a garrison into Nantes, offering pledges to the duchess and also to De Rieux that they would evacuate the town in three months, or even in six days, after being requested to give it up. The state of Britanny at the time was very miserable, and the peasantry, finding their country to be a mere bone of contention between France and England, rose in some places in revolt, refusing to pay the hearth money imposed by the duchess. They declared that they would choose a duke and duchess of their own, and obey no foreign masters. A regular pitched battle took place between them and the English on the lands of the Lords of Rohan and Quintin, in which 400 villeins were killed and 300 taken. But of course this did not mend matters. A country must have a settled government, and a strong government, before citizens can live in peace ; and the evils of a hostile occupation can hardly be mitigated by the antidote of a peasant war. The question who was to rule the duchy remained yet to be decided, but it was nearer solution than men thought.

As the conferences at Boulogne and Calais gave no hope of a favourable result, the king sent fresh troops to Britanny under the command of Lord Daubeney, and a fleet under that of Lord Willoughby de Broke. As a pledge for the repayment of his expenses, he bargained that the town of Morlaix should be put into his hands, and the duchess agreed to pay him 6000 crowns a year for the privilege of levying the *gabelles* and customs as usual during his occupation of it. The result seems to have been that, though the sittings of the congress were broken off as hopeless, the French for a time forbore to

molest Britanny further. Charles, indeed, assembled a
great army and drew near to the confines of the duchy;
but on a careful survey of the situation he desisted from
a new invasion. Leaving the strongholds he had gained
well garrisoned, he withdrew his other forces on the 15th
of August and agreed to an armistice; while on the
other hand Henry made a treaty with Maximilian (11th
September) for the defence alike of Britanny and of
Burgundy against any attack on his part.

The prospect of vindicating successfully the independence of the duchy had in fact considerably improved.
De Rieux and the duchess now fully understood each
other; and a sense of common interest had drawn together England, Spain, and Burgundy to support them
more effectually than they had done hitherto. Henry
sent the Garter to Maximilian, advising him to press on
his marriage with the Duchess Anne; and Ferdinand
and Isabella, beginning to doubt the feasibility of marrying her to their son, also expressed themselves in favour
of the match. And as the duchess herself was willing
to accept him, it was not long before the knot was tied,
or seemed to be so, to all intents and purposes. Maximilian, it is true, found a difficulty in leaving the Low
Countries, and part of his design seems to have been to
act with secrecy. He determined to marry the duchess
by proxy, and sent Count Nassau to Britanny to act in
his stead. The marriage was not only celebrated in
this manner, but was even considered to have been con-
summated by the strange ceremony of the ambassador
inserting his leg, stripped naked to the knee, between the
sheets in presence of witnesses; so that the duchess, who
had not even yet completed her fourteenth year, was now

to be regarded as the actual wife of Maximilian. For a time the fact was carefully concealed; but early in the year 1491 Anne publicly assumed the title of Queen of the Romans.

The King of the Romans was a king without a kingdom, and though his son's duchy of Burgundy and earldom of Flanders were, even since the days of Charles the Bold, almost as good as the kingdom of France, he had practically little command over their resources. Anne, on the other hand, had been hitherto little better than a duchess without a duchy; and the marriage was even more a nullity, as the reputed husband and wife had not yet even seen each other. But the fact that it had taken place put matters on a new footing entirely; for unless it could be annulled before the parties came together, it must be held practically valid. And while the dominions of the husband and the wife lay too far apart to be of great assistance to each other against the common enemy which lay between them, England, having the command of the sea, could strengthen both, and through them could easily harass France on both sides. Spain too, if it saw fit, could make a diversion at the same time in the south; so that France would be surrounded by enemies. Charles VIII. and his Council were fully alive to the danger; and though he had so lately found it necessary to pause in his aggressive policy, and in fact had made a truce with Britanny, he now made secret arrangements to violate his engagement and fall upon the duchy by surprise.

The weak point in the pacification by which De Rieux had been reconciled to the duchess was that the Sieur d'Albret was practically thrown over. When his pro-

posal to marry the duchess was no longer supported
even by De Rieux, it was clear that he could only be
trusted, at the utmost, to stand neutral. And this he
apparently did until the date of the marriage with
Maximilian; for he was such an old enemy of France in
these matters that he could not easily ally himself with
Charles VIII. against the cause of Breton independence.
But besides disappointment at the duchess's marriage
with Maximilian, he cherished a fancied claim by inheritance to one-third of the duchy, from which he saw
himself effectually barred under the new state of matters.
And thus he lent himself as a ready tool to King Charles,
who, it was surely no secret, had been another of his
rivals in seeking to become Anne's husband; for alike in
claiming rights of wardship and in invading her country
Charles had apparently all along intended to secure his
interests there in the last resort by marriage, notwithstanding his engagement, under the treaty of Arras, to
marry Maximilian's daughter.

D'Albret accordingly made a secret bargain with the
French king to deliver up to him the important city of
Nantes, the old and favourite residence of the Dukes of
Britanny. The terms which he exacted for this service
were costly enough to Charles, but the latter had no
difficulty in accepting them, undertaking that, as soon
as the city was delivered, it should be placed in the
hands of the Duke of Bourbon until D'Albret's demands
were satisfied. D'Albret fulfilled his compact to the
uttermost. He got a garrison on whom he could rely
introduced into the castle, and Charles having sent
thither the Duke of Bourbon, the place was surrendered
to him. Having satisfied D'Albret, he next went thither

himself, took the submissions of the town and castle on
the 4th of April, remained there a week, and after putting
in a garrison, returned into Touraine.

An almost incredible statement occurs in a letter
written at this time to the Pope by the Bishop of Concordia from Tours. "The French," he writes, "are informed that the King of the Romans, on hearing of the
capture of Nantes, did not much care about it, and that
he wishes for peace with his son-in-law (Charles VIII.),
and to return to Hungary." He had, indeed, involved
himself in too many matters to be of much assistance
to Britanny; for in the preceding year he had been a
candidate for the Crown of Hungary, and was now at
war with the candidate actually elected, Ladislaus, King
of Bohemia. But he did write to his father, the emperor,
and other princes of Germany for aid in the recovery of
Nantes, and at a diet held at Nuremberg 12,000 lance-
knights were granted to him for the purpose. Further,
he sent to England to ask aid of Henry on promise to
repay expenses. Britanny, however, was practically
lost already. Maximilian could not go thither himself.
The duchess was thinking of going to him. Arrangements for the pay of auxiliaries were breaking down.
The French took Redon, won Concarneau from the
English, and proceeded to besiege Rennes, the only town
that was able to offer them anything like effective resistance; and towards the close of the year, on the 15th of
November, while Charles himself lay in the suburbs
with his army, the duchess was compelled to make a
temporary arrangement with him, by which she agreed
that the city should be made neutral and placed in the
hands of the Prince of Orange to keep, pending some

final decision by arbitrators appointed to examine the whole controversy between them.

On this Charles withdrew his army, all but the men left to garrison the different towns, and retired into Touraine.   But fifteen days later Anne went to meet him at Langeais, and there, on the 6th of December, repudiating her unreal union with Maximilian, she married him and became Queen of France.   A papal dispensation had been procured beforehand, not to annul the ceremony of the "bootless calf" or the pre-contract of Charles himself with Maximilian's daughter, but simply for the matter of consanguinity between the parties ; and even in this respect it was inadequate to meet the case.   But a new dispensation, granted on the 15th of December, supplied all that was wanting, and it was vain to protest against an accomplished fact.   From that time forward the duchy of Britanny was merged in the Crown of France.

CHAPTER VI

THE WAR WITH FRANCE

So all the money spent and lives lost to preserve the independence of Britanny had been thrown away. The disappointment was undoubtedly severe both to the English people and to their king; nor was it greatly mitigated by the attitude or circumstances of those who should have shared the mortification along with them. For though Ferdinand and Isabella may have had their own unpleasant reflections on the event, even in the midst of their triumph at the conquest of Granada, which took place at that very time, they were still too much occupied in the south of Spain to care much about the north of France. While as for Maximilian, who had most to complain of, having been doubly, indeed trebly duped (for he had been cheated of a wife, and also of a duchy, by the very same act by which his daughter had been cheated of a husband); he too had far-off interests to defend which would make it difficult for him to act with energy.

Henry, however, had not laid his plans so badly that serious loss could overwhelm all his calculations. From the first he had counted the cost of a possible breach with France, and had determined not to commit himself to it without reasonable security for his indemnification. Something of this we have seen already as regards the assistance he had given to Britanny. But if that had been all, he had now practically lost his securities; for Concarneau had been already wrested from the English before the annexation of Britanny, and it is clear there could have been no hope of defending Morlaix, though at what precise date and under what circumstances it was given up we do not find recorded. The utmost that could be done in Britanny now was to land men, ravage the country, and carry off booty—a course which was actually pursued in the summer of 1491 both in Britanny and Normandy. As to securing a permanent position in the country there does not seem to have been a thought.

But we must not confine our view to the question between France and Britanny if we would understand the scope of Henry's policy. War was a thing that he himself would rather have avoided, and even where it made for his own interest and for that of England, he certainly did not wish to enter upon it without allies. We must, however, go back a few years to explain how he was led into the matter, and how he endeavoured to protect himself from loss.

Having secured his throne to some extent by his marriage with Elizabeth of York, the birth of his son, Prince Arthur, in September 1486 was an additional source of strength to him—not merely because his children would unite the claims both of York and Lancaster, but because they would be a useful means of strengthening foreign alliances. And the young prince could hardly have been more than a twelvemonth old

when a proposal was made by Henry to Ferdinand and
Isabella of Spain for his marriage, as soon as he should
reach a suitable age, to their infant daughter Katharine,
who was just nine months older. The Spanish sovereigns,
engaged in consolidating their power in the Peninsula as
Henry was in strengthening his own position in England,
considered that such an alliance might be for their
mutual benefit, and sent a special envoy commissioned
among other things to negotiate the match in concert
with their resident ambassador, De Puebla. He arrived
in London on the 1st of June, and had audience of the
king along with De Puebla three days later, at which
audience, as the latter informed Ferdinand, Henry
opened his eyes wide with joy and broke into a *Te Deum
laudamus* when he found that they were armed with
powers to conclude the alliance. Particulars were left
to be discussed between the Spanish commissioners and
others named by Henry, and after a good deal of con
ference a formal agreement for the marriage was drawn
up on the 7th of July. This, however, was only a
general statement of conditions as a basis for further
negotiation; and an English embassy was to be despatched
to Spain to make more complete arrangements.

The reason why the matter could not be fully concluded in England was that the Spanish ambassadors
had been instructed to demand so high a price for the
alliance that the English commissioners, however unwilling to break off, could not possibly agree to it. Henry
was to bind himself never to aid the King of France in
war, but to make war upon him whenever Ferdinand
and Isabella did so, and never to make peace or truce
with him till they did; in return for which engagement

the Spanish sovereigns only promised not to make peace with France without including England. The disparity of conditions was obvious, but it seems to have been assumed as a matter of course that England had much more need of the help of Spain than Spain could have of that of England. Nor did the English commissioners dispute the assumption. They only pointed out that there was no reciprocity, and that it was very inexpedient, in any case, to put such terms into writing. Besides, the King of England had notoriously been indebted to the French king for most important favours, and it would not be honourable for him to insert a clause expressly aimed against France. The things Ferdinand and Isabella required Henry to do, said the English commissioners, might be justified when done far better than they could be when written as specific pledges. De Puebla was not satisfied with this Jesuitical answer; and the English, to content him, took a mass-book and swore before a crucifix that it was the will and intention of Henry first to conclude the alliance and the marriage, and afterwards to make war upon France at the bidding of Ferdinand and Isabella. Henry afterwards told the Spanish ambassadors he had been informed of the taking of this oath, and that he quite agreed to it. He seemed entirely the servant of the Spanish sovereigns, whose names he never mentioned without taking off his bonnet, with conventional courtesy, in the presence of their representatives.

This, it should be mentioned, was at the time of Lord Woodville's unauthorised expedition to Britanny, when the feeling against France, even within his own kingdom, was such as Henry found it very difficult to control.

But, as shown already, he had just extended the truce
with that country to January 1490, and in the interval
of eighteen months many things might occur ; but he was
not going to make war before that date, at all events,
and not after it without a very clear understanding with
the Spanish sovereigns. Such an understanding, however, he was himself very anxious to arrive at after the
battle of St. Aubin and the death of the Duke of Britanny. Early in October he sent new proposals to Ferdinand touching France, and pressed for an immediate
answer, and in December he sent Dr. Thomas Savage
and Sir Richard Nanfan to Spain with full power to
conclude both the political alliance and the marriage
treaty. Meanwhile Ferdinand and Isabella had sent, in
answer to the remonstrances of their own ambassador,
some slight modifications of their original instructions,
and of the terms on which they insisted as necessary to
the treaty.

The great object of the Spanish sovereigns was to
recover from France the counties of Roussillon and
Cerdagne, a small patch of territory at the eastern end
of the Pyrenees, which formed the key to Catalonia,
and which had been mortgaged by Ferdinand's father to
Louis XI. And it was hoped that Henry would enable
them to achieve that object, as an alliance with the
two powerful kingdoms of Castile and Arragon would
strengthen his own weak position on the throne. Such
an alliance, indeed, was sure to be popular in England,
being quite in accordance with the traditions of national
policy ; and if it involved a breach with France it might
not be the less popular on that account. So, as the
possibility of the proposed marriage actually taking place

was yet a long way off, the Spanish sovereigns resolved
to see what price Henry was prepared to pay for it;
and their first demand was, as we have seen, nothing
less than that the resources of England should be at
their absolute control for the purpose of making war on
France whenever they pleased to do so. They professed
not to understand the objections raised to this in England,
seeing that they only asked Henry to put in writing
what he had actually declared to their ambassador in
words; but to give a greater appearance of reciprocity,
they would consent to Henry binding himself to make
war at the request of Spain, as the Spanish sovereigns
would at the request of England, neither party to make
peace unless France should give up to England the
duchies of Guienne and Normandy, or to Spain the
counties of Roussillon and Cerdagne. In the former
case Henry was to be free to make a separate peace, in
the latter Ferdinand and Isabella. It is needless to say
that the terms were utterly unequal, as France could be
much more easily induced to give up a petty district in
the Pyrenees than two such important provinces as
Guienne and Normandy. Nor does it appear that Henry
ever authorised his ambassadors to accept such terms
Yet when Dr. Savage and Sir Richard Nanfan reached
the Spanish Court at Medina del Campo in March 1489,
it was actually embodied in a treaty between the two
countries. Care was taken, indeed, that the obligations
which it imposed upon Henry should be only conditional;
for, first, his existing truce with France was to be
respected till January 1490; and secondly, at the
expiration of that truce (unless England found herself
immediately involved in war), either party should be at

liberty to conclude a new truce with France, including
the other in it. So that in fact it was England, not
Spain, that thus held the key of the position; for if
England found herself at war in January 1490, Spain
was bound to aid her, at least till Roussillon and Cerdagne were restored; but if England was not at war at
that date, either she or Spain could conclude a new truce
provided the other party were included.

Still the state of matters, in view of actual war
breaking out, was not favourable to England; for the
French king, if at all hard pressed, could easily give up
Roussillon and Cerdagne to Spain and so dissolve the
alliance. But though the treaty was ratified by Ferdinand and Isabella at Medina del Campo, it had still to
be ratified by Henry, and until that was done nothing
was yet concluded. Meanwhile England was giving real
assistance both to Britanny and to Maximilian against
France without violating the existing truce; and things
were going on so far well that Henry thought he might
fairly ask for some new stipulations with regard to the
marriage, which, however, were refused. Then came
the treaty of Frankfort, which showed the weakness of
Maximilian; and its acceptance by Britanny, which
showed the weakness of the Duchess Anne. There was
no need of Henry's ratification just then to bind Ferdinand to act along with him; for it was his clear interest
to do so. And the treaty remained unratified by England
till the 20th of September 1490, a year and a half after
its ratification by the Spanish sovereigns at Medina,
when the situation had very considerably changed, and
owing to the failure of Chieregato's attempts at mediation, England found herself actually at war with France

—or at least upon the brink of it, for a truce was presently made for the winter months—and so was immediately entitled to call upon Ferdinand and Isabella for assistance. But when he did so he had other proposals to lay before the Spanish sovereigns at the same time.

Meanwhile he was carefully observing all his engagements, while arming for a not far distant struggle. Throughout the year 1489, while his original truce with France still lasted, he was continually impressing soldiers and seamen, not for aggressive purposes, but for defence of the duchy. So also during 1490 he sent out various commissions of array against invasion and for the defence of Calais, and on the 11th of September— just when the peace negotiations of Chieregato had definitively failed—he concluded, first, a treaty with Maximilian for the defence of Britanny and for mutual aid against the common enemy. This was followed by a secret compact between them, dated one day later, by which each bound himself to declare open hostility to France and to make actual war upon it at his own expense within the next three years, with a proviso that Ferdinand and Isabella should be included in these arrangements if they chose. Thus a foundation was laid for a larger and stronger alliance than that which previously existed between England and Spain alone, and proclamation was made immediately afterwards (on the 17th of September) of a league between the three powers —England, Spain, and the King of the Romans—for mutual defence against France. This undoubtedly gratified the war spirit in England, and Henry, when three days later he ratified the treaty of Medina del Campo, drew up and signed at the same time another treaty with Spain, for the purpose of including all the three allies under the same obligations.

Now this new treaty, which was conveyed to Spain along with the ratification of the other, was certainly more favourable to Henry as regards reciprocity; but it was a much more definite arrangement altogether, and one which could not reasonably be objected to by an ally who really intended to keep faith. It was arranged with Ferdinand and Isabella, just as it had been with Maximilian, that if France should invade the territory either of England, Spain, or Britanny, and if either Henry or Ferdinand should proclaim war against France in consequence, and engage in actual hostilities, the other should be bound, a year after being requested so to do, to invade France at his own expense. It was further stipulated that, as the French king had actually usurped territories belonging to Spain, England, and Britanny, the English and Spanish sovereigns should declare war against him within three years, and invade France personally, with armies sufficient to reconquer the territories taken from them; that they should carry on the war without interruption for two years, and that neither should discontinue it *within that time* without the consent of the other; unless *not only* Spain should recover Roussillon and Cerdagne, but England also should regain Normandy and Guienne. Thus England would no longer be bound to fight merely for the benefit of Ferdinand and Isabella, only to be left in the lurch as soon as they had recovered Roussillon and Cerdagne. If the alliance against France was to be effective, Henry naturally asked that it should be cordial and reciprocal.

But would Ferdinand and Isabella accept this new

treaty when they had already got Henry committed to one more to their advantage? That remained to be seen. The document was at least a test of their sincerity, as to which Henry may well have had misgivings. No separate peace could be made by either party if this new treaty was accepted. But Ferdinand, as a matter of fact, had been making some efforts to arrive at a separate peace already. Secret messengers had passed between the two Courts with proposals for an arrangement involving the abandonment of Britanny if Charles would marry Joanna, second daughter of the Spanish sovereigns. But a peace between France and England Ferdinand sought by all means to oppose, and when Chieregato was endeavouring to negotiate it he urged his ambassador at Rome to get the Pope to recall the nuncio's colleague, Flores, and to persuade his Holiness that mediation between France and Spain was much more important than between France and England, for peace between the latter two powers would immediately follow if France and Spain were reconciled. Henry perhaps did not know the full extent of Ferdinand's double-dealing. But he knew that the Spanish ambassadors in Britanny were at that very moment ostensibly disobeying the instructions they had received, and had just asked him to excuse them to their own sovereigns, for reasons with which he professed to be satisfied, for withdrawing the Spanish forces from the duchy. They would not be wanted, the ambassadors urged, during the winter, as a truce had been agreed to, but they would be sent back in spring.

It is needless to say that the new treaty was not accepted by Spain; and for a thousand plausible reasons

the troops were not sent back.   Before the return of
spring Nantes had fallen.   The Spanish sovereigns were
very sorry, and intended to redress the wrong.   They
professed to regard the affair as their own, but still they
had no means of immediate action, and must trust to
Henry and Maximilian, who were nearer at hand.   They
were most urgent that Henry should pour fresh troops
into the duchy and make war upon France with all his
power; and as soon as they themselves had secured
their conquests in Granada they would do their utmost
to assist.   Henry must have seen pretty clearly how
little help he was likely to get from Spain ; but he was
already involved in the responsibilities of war, and was
busy still with commissions of array, raising men to repel
invasion, which was expected all through the spring,
and impressing sailors for a fleet to fight the king's
enemies at sea.   In May he received an application from
Maximilian and Anne, as King and Queen of the Romans,
asking aid against the French and promising repayment
of expenses.   In July, having apparently obtained the
sanction of a Great Council to a step which was, strictly
speaking, illegal, he appointed commissioners throughout the country for a "benevolence" towards the war.
In October he called Parliament together, and declaring
to them his intention of invading France in person,
obtained further a grant of two-fifteenths and tenths to
furnish the expedition properly.   And having so far
prepared for the struggle, he next month made another
effort to fix Ferdinand to some precise terms of co-opera-
tion.   On the 22d of November he drew up two new
treaties with Spain, the one binding both parties
formally to declare war against France before the 15th

H

of April following, and to begin actual hostilities by the
15th of June at latest; the other binding Ferdinand and
Isabella to send their daughter Katharine to England as
soon as Prince Arthur should complete his fourteenth
year, and to pay the stipulated dowry of 200,000 crowns
for her.   Thus war and matrimony were wont to go
hand in hand, the one a pledge for the other.

Matrimony, however, had the advantage of war as
regards France; for exactly a fortnight after this treaty
was drawn up the Duchess Anne was married to Charles
VIII., and the independence of Britanny was gone past
recovery.   Past all recovery—that, at least, was plain;
and however little men might relish the fact, one great
cause for the war had already disappeared.   True, the
injury might be avenged; but what prince was prepared
to do so?   Not Ferdinand and Isabella, who made no
haste to sign the new treaty, or even to fulfil the old;
for they were still busy with the Moors in Granada.
Not even Maximilian, the most deeply injured of all;
for though he had by this time succeeded in the east
of Europe and secured his right to the archduchy of
Austria, he was still crippled in his resources.   Austria
was exhausted, and could yield him nothing; the Low
Countries were not even yet obedient to him.   Henry
alone was prepared, and intended to fulfil his engagements.   He, however, gave both Ferdinand and Maximilian every opportunity of doing so, and delayed his
own expedition against France as long as he safely could
to enable them to co-operate.   At last, when the best
part of the year 1492 had already passed, he issued pro-
·nations on the 2d of August for every one able to serve
in war to be ready at an hour's warning.   Later in the

month, to assist Maximilian as well as himself, he sent
a fleet under Sir Edward Poynings to besiege Sluys in
concert with troops by land brought by Albert, Duke of
Saxony, and their operations were so effectual that in
about a couple of months the town with its two castles
surrendered, the former to the Duke of Saxony, the
latter to Sir Edward Poynings.

Even the siege of this town, quite apart from its
surrender, did much to assist the war against France ;
for Sluys was not only the heart of the rebellion against
Maximilian's authority, but was also a nest of pirates
checking the approaches to Antwerp, and indeed to
the whole of Brabant and the Low Countries generally.
The siege was still going on in September when the
king, having collected a large army in London, marched
towards the sea-side.   It is said he received letters from
France offering terms when on his way to Sandwich,
but of this of course no one then knew.   He crossed to
Calais on the 6th of October—no doubt to the great
astonishment of many, that he would begin an invasion
so very late in the year.   Here ambassadors that he had
sent to Maximilian returned from Flanders with the
unpleasant information (we may be sure not unexpected
by the king) that the King of the Romans was quite
unprepared to join in an expedition against France.
His will was good, but neither Austria nor Flanders
provided him with the means of action, and he must
leave Henry to effect what he could by himself.
Rumours too could not fail to arrive that Ferdinand
and Isabella, instead of being faithful to England, were
at that very moment once more negotiating a separate
peace with France, and would have closed the bargain if

Charles would have consented readily to grant them what they had so much desired. Still the army was not disheartened, and presently sat down before Boulogne.

The town was well fortified, and could hardly have been taken without much bloodshed. For some time the English battered the walls, and in the course of their operations they lost one brave captain, Sir John Savage. But before matters had gone very far, proposals for peace, which the Sieur d'Esquerdes had been authorised to make, were laid before the captains of the English army ; who, considering the terms, the time of year, the difficulty of victualling the forces in winter, and the hopelessness of getting aid from any ally, advised the king to accept them. Charles, in fact, agreed to pay the whole debt, which was to have fallen on Maximilian, amounting to 620,000 crowns, due to the king from Anne of Britanny for his assistance in the defence of the duchy, and two years' arrears of the pension promised by Louis XI. to Edward IV. at the peace of Amiens,—altogether 745,000 crowns, which he engaged to discharge at the rate of 50,000 francs a year.[1] The terms were accepted, and a treaty was accordingly signed at Etaples on the 3d of November which was confirmed by Charles three days later. The English army then withdrew to Calais, and soon after returned to England.

[1] The franc of those days seems to have been an obsolete gold coin of the value of twenty silver sols, or about six shillings sterling. But in purchasing power it was probably equal to more than £3 of our present money, so that each yearly payment was equivalent to upwards of £150,000 nowadays. The crown, or *écu d'or*, was worth generally between ten and eleven shillings sterling, and the whole indemnity must have been equivalent to three and a half or four millions of English money at the present day.

The peace was evidently made upon the model of the peace of Amiens. Charles VIII. only followed the policy of his father in buying off English aggression. For however hopeless, from an English statesman's point of view, might be the project of reconquering France, the landing of a foreign enemy would have stirred up internal commotions in a kingdom which it had been the chief aim, both of Louis and of Charles, to consolidate and strengthen. It would, moreover, have altogether frustrated a design on which Charles had already set his heart—the invasion of Italy. So he was glad, like his father, to buy a peace with England. He had not the same occasion to come immediately to terms with Ferdinand, who gained little by his separate negotiation with France until some time after the peace with England had been settled; but Charles at length agreed also to his demand for the restoration of Roussillon and Cerdagne.

Henry had strictly fulfilled his engagements to all foreign princes; but the peace was scarcely popular with his own subjects, who had been heavily taxed for what was not a war, nor even much of a campaign, merely to fill the king's coffers. Indeed some of the captains in the army had mortgaged their estates to supply him with money for the expedition, hoping that it would have been a great opportunity for themselves to "win their spurs." There could be no doubt, however, that it was for the best interests of England as well as of France that war between them should cease; and even against the will of his people Henry had secured their good.

CHAPTER VII

No politician who had marked Henry's progress hitherto could doubt that he had shown remarkable skill and patience in the treatment of very serious difficulties. For a ruler seated on an unsteady throne it was not a very agreeable experience, first to be dragged into war against his will, then to find everything lost that he had been fighting for, and lastly to be deserted by all his allies when about to exact compensation for the loss. But the very fact that he had at length won the game single-handed gave him a position that he had not enjoyed before. He had become really independent of foreign potentates. France had been content to buy his friendship, and he had no need now to pay an exorbitant price for that of Spain. His own subjects, moreover, had been taught a lesson that if they must have war they must pay for it, and that the extent of their indulgence in that pastime might after all be limited. The soldiers whom he had brought before Boulogne had seen the strength of a place which the enemy had received very long notice to fortify against invasion, and they could not but feel the force of the reasons given by their own leaders in the memorial to the king for accepting

Charles's terms. For there were now no great vassals of the French Crown, as in former days, to assist England in the invasion; there were no allies ready, even at the eleventh hour, to fulfil their solemn engagements. That the king, under those circumstances, had actually razed some fortresses in Picardy; that he had reduced Sluys and other towns to Maximilian and freed English commerce with the Low Countries from further molestation; and that finally he had drawn a larger tribute from France than any English king had done before—results like these were by no means insignificant. He had benefited every one of his allies without receiving any aid from them, and he was free from any obligation to prosecute an expensive war in future.

At the same time the result, as we have seen, occasioned naturally enough some disappointments at home, and it was not yet clear to foreign princes that he had come to the end of his difficulties. If he had been able, or even disposed, to repeat the achievements of Henry V. in France, he would have impressed the world differently. He might have drained off some domestic discontent into the favourite channel of martial ardour; and allies like Maximilian would probably have remained firm until he began to meet with serious disaster. But when, instead of conquest, he was content with a mere settlement of expenses; when allies whom he had sufficiently benefited saw that there was nothing more to be got out of him; when subjects who had been heavily taxed saw no return for their money except some security for peace,—the unquiet spirits at home and abroad began to think they might yet raise up trouble for a king so pacifically inclined. Foreign princes too were naturally

lukewarm towards a sovereign who now showed himself
independent of them.   Ferdinand and Isabella had, as a
result of Henry's campaign, got all they wanted out of
France ; and having for the present no further need
of his friendship, were endeavouring now to discover
whether Henry could easily sustain the loss of theirs.
And in this interesting investigation they were soon
afterwards followed by those who were even more indebted to Henry than themselves—Maximilian, King of
the Romans, and his son Philip, Archduke of Austria.

It is really in this light that the encouragement given
to Perkin Warbeck by different princes ought to be
regarded.   A true prince of the House of York no
doubt would have been a more valuable piece on the
political chess-board ; but an impostor was a very useful
pawn that might have been exchanged, if successful, for
a man of more importance.   And it required no particular trouble to set the impostor up.   He had already
appeared on the scene before Henry's expedition to
Boulogne.   He had not, as commonly supposed, received
an elaborate training from Margaret, Duchess of Burgundy, for he had personated the second son of Edward
IV. long before he visited her Court.   So far as we can
tell, his first patrons were not men of mark in the
political world at all.   It was in the congenial atmo-
sphere of Ireland that he was first started on his adventures ; and there seems no great reason to question his
own confession that it was the Irish people rather than
himself who determined the character he was to personate, though it may be that cunning persons were at the
bottom of the plot.   He was really a native of Tournay,
who, after leading a roving life, had entered the service of

a Breton merchant named Pregent Meno, and had gone on a trading voyage to Cork, where he disembarked and showed himself in silk array, having dressed himself up, no doubt, in the cloths in which his master traded. The citizens of Cork were attracted by the appearance of the stranger, who, they had not a doubt, must be some very distinguished person. Was he not the Earl of Warwick? The sympathies of the Irish were always with the House of York, and they had a particular regard for the memory of Warwick's father, the Duke of Clarence, who had been Viceroy and was born at Dublin. Perkin, perhaps not meaning at the outset to attempt a gigantic imposture, denied that he was the Earl of Warwick; yet such was the zeal of his friends to get up a political fiction that he had to deny it before the Mayor of Cork on oath, else his career would have been passed under a different name from that which he ultimately adopted.

If he was not Warwick, his Irish friends then surmised that he must be a bastard son of Richard III. But this too he denied; and his denial was the more readily accepted because it was shrewdly suspected that King Richard's bastard son was in the hands of the King of England. Another theory was therefore devised which could not be refuted in the same manner. The stranger must be Richard, Duke of York, younger son of Edward IV.; and they urged him not to be afraid to assume the character, for they would protect him against the power of the King of England, and they were quite sure the Earls of Desmond and Kildare would support him also. Won by these assurances, Perkin entered on the perilous path which led him ultimately to the scaffold.

Desmond certainly did adhere to him and Kildare as well, though the latter, who was still Lord Deputy (it was not three years, perhaps not more than two, since Sir Richard Edgecombe had taken his fealty), supported him in a manner which enabled him plausibly to disavow it afterwards. Not much seems to have come of the affair in Ireland itself; but the rumour that the Duke of York was still alive was sent abroad to other countries, particularly to France and Scotland. Messengers from Desmond and the reputed son of Edward IV. arrived at the Scotch Court in March 1492, and a little before Henry's invasion of France, Charles VIII. sent over to Ireland Stephen Frion, who had lately been Henry VII.'s French secretary, but had deserted or been dismissed his service, to ask the adventurer to come and live in France. Perkin readily accepted the invitation, was received at the French Court as a foreign prince, and had a guard of honour assigned him. A number of disaffected Yorkists also came over from England to join him. But on peace being made, Charles had to dismiss the pretender, who then betook himself to the Low Countries with the Yorkist exiles, he and they being alike sure of a cordial reception from the Lady Margaret, Duchess-dowager of Burgundy — Henry's Juno, as she was called, from her inveterate hatred and intrigues against him. From her it was only natural that he should receive some training in Court manners, and especially (as it suited her policy to acknowledge him as a nephew) that she should instruct him well in the pedigree and descent of the House of York, which is just what the early writer Polydore Vergil informs us that she did. But the story of the education he received from her has been clearly exaggerated by Lord Bacon and by most historians after him, whose accounts certainly suggest that she told him family secrets, which in her absènce from England she had hardly much opportunity of knowing herself.[1]

This open encouragement given abroad to a pretender to the English throne was naturally a trial to Henry's pacific policy. But Juno was in the clouds and could not be got hold of. She was not a sovereign princess, but only a duchess-dowager, living on the lands of her jointure under the protection of her husband's grandson, Philip of Austria. Henry must therefore address his remonstrances to him; and he sent over Sir Edward Poynings, to whose services at Sluys the Flemings were much indebted, and Dr. Warham, afterwards Archbishop of Canterbury, to the Low Countries with that object. The Archduke Philip was only fifteen years old, and his Council, influenced no doubt partly by Margaret herself, but probably still more by the French party in Flanders, replied that he was anxious to cultivate the best possible terms with England, but that the dowager was free to do as she pleased within her own lands. This practically

---

[1] "Then she informed him of all the circumstances and partic- ulars that concerned the person of Richard, Duke of York, which he was to act; describing unto him the personages, lineaments, and features of the king and queen, his pretended parents, and of his brother and sisters, and divers others that were nearest him in childhood, together with all passages, some secret, some common, that were fit for a child's memory, until the death of King Edward. Then she added the particulars of the time from the king's death until he and his brother were committed to the Tower, as well during the time he was abroad as while he was in sanctuary."— Pacon's *Henry VII.* Margaret of Burgundy paid a visit to England in 1480, but she had no special knowledge of the tragic history of the year 1483.

meant that Henry must look to himself in case any
hostile expedition should be secretly fitted out in the
Low Countries and land on the English coast. Henry
might fairly have answered by a declaration of war with
Flanders—a course to which he was naturally averse,
and from which he allowed himself to be dissuaded by
the Spanish ambassador. So he only wrote to trusty
men to be prepared to serve him at a day's warning for
the defence of the kingdom. But he determined at the
same time that the unfriendly treatment he had received
from the Flemings should be visited on themselves; and
since they made him so bad a return for freeing their
commerce from molestation, he recalled the merchant
adventurers from Antwerp, forbade commercial intercourse with Flanders, and proposed to set up a mart for
English cloth at Calais.

The immediate result of course was a great deal of
inconvenience to the merchants of England as well as of
the Netherlands—in fact, rather more to the former
than to the latter. For it was presently discovered that
a set of aliens in the very heart of London—the merchants
of the Hanse, commonly called, from their place of business, the merchants of the Steelyard—were by their
charters exempt from the prohibition, and carried on
freely the traffic from which English merchants were
excluded. The result was a riot in the city, which was
with difficulty appeased; while the pressure put upon
the Flemings did not prevent Perkin from receiving
shelter and support in the Low Countries for about two
years and a half. The attempt to divert English commerce from the Low Countries was hopeless, and the
Archduke's Council, conscious that England could not

afford to quarrel with Flanders, continued the same irritating policy of pretended friendliness. Maximilian also, who on the death of his father, Frederic, in 1493 had come to be recognised as emperor (though his title strictly was still only King of the Romans), forgetful of repeated benefits at Henry's hands, was quite zealous in favour of the pretender; and Henry knew long before it was launched that an expedition was being prepared in the Low Countries for the invasion of England.

It would probably have sailed two years earlier than it did but for the difficulty Maximilian commonly found in obtaining supplies; for the pretender could not look for much help from any other quarter. Soon after his arrival in those parts he had written to Queen Isabella of Spain, setting forth his claims as Duke of York, and giving an account of his adventures; but the letter was simply laid aside, docketed by the Spanish Secretary of State as "from Richard, who calls himself King of England." Ferdinand and Isabella were too wise to have anything to do with him. The French king offered Henry the benefit of his navy in case of any hostile attempt against England; but Henry replied that as to the matter of the *garçon*, as he called him, there was no need of any special precautions—it was quite well known in England that he was the son of a boatman in Tournay. Henry, no doubt, looked upon his pretensions with very genuine contempt, while foreign princes, friendly and unfriendly, tried to magnify their importance as a possible source of disturbance. But Henry knew that real danger could only come from conspiracy at home in aid of an invasion, and he was sufficiently on his guard against being dispossessed of his throne in the way he had dispossessed King Richard.

But the caution of Henry and the impecuniosity of Maximilian are in themselves scarcely sufficient explanation of the fact that a pretender to the English throne should have lain two and a half years in Flanders, encouraged openly by a Duchess-dowager of Burgundy and secretly by the Archduke Philip's Council, without making any attempt to realise his pretensions. The fact is that European princes were at this time engrossed with matters of much greater consequence. It was during those two years and a half that Charles VIII. had made his famous expedition into Italy, when it was said that his soldiers had come merely with chalk in their hands to mark up their lodgings. At his approach one King of Naples had abdicated, and his successor had been obliged to fly. In fact, he was welcomed everywhere as the deliverer of Italy, and particularly of Naples, from intolerable tyranny and misgovernment. Yet, unconscious of the cause to which his success was due, he seemed to think himself not a liberator, but a conqueror, and alienated the hearts of the Italians almost as soon as he had won them; with the result that he was nearly locked up in the peninsula by the very same princes who had invited him into it. Chief of these was the scheming Ludovico Maria Sforza, called by the Italians "the Moor," uncle of the Duke of Milan and regent of the duchy, who assured him that Venice would stand neutral, and that the only opposition he had to look for was in seeking to make good his claim to Naples. Before he had gone far this Ludovico had become Duke of Milan himself by the very suspicious death of his nephew, whom he had kept imprisoned at Pavia. But in the following spring the Pope, the Duke of Milan, and the Venetian republic were all Charles's enemies, and had formed a league against him with Maximilian and Ferdinand of Spain.

Neither had Henry in England been indifferent to the affairs of Italy. Far off as he was, he had taken some pains to establish friendly relations with the Arragonese Kings of Naples—no doubt as a kind of check on France if Charles should not be faithful to his engagements. Just after the treaty of Etaples he had sent the Garter to Alfonso, Duke of Calabria, who became King of Naples by his father's death before Charles VIII.'s invasion. He had also cultivated the most cordial relations with Milan, and had even listened to a proposal for marrying the young Duke Galeazzo Maria Sforza to a daughter of Edward IV. and sister of his own queen. If in these matters his policy bore little fruit it was not for want of careful and intelligent watching of the affairs of Italy. "In many things," wrote a Milanese envoy in London to Ludovico Sforza a year or two later, "in many things I know this sovereign to be admirably well informed, but above all because he is most thoroughly acquainted with the affairs of Italy, and receives especial information of every event. He is no less conversant with your own personal attributes and those of your duchy than the King of France; and when the King of France went into Italy the King of England sent with him a herald of his own called Richmond, a sage man who saw everything, until his return. Then the merchants, most especially the Florentines, never cease giving the King of England advices."

It was by this continual watchfulness, studying the
world far and near, and keeping himself perfectly informed at all times of the internal state of other countries
as well as his own, and their relations towards each other,
that Henry, the most pacific prince that ever reigned,
ere long made his value as an ally felt by wise sovereigns
over the whole of Europe.   But the conviction that he
was firmly seated on his throne was by no means even
yet universal, and there were sovereigns far from wise,
like Maximilian, King of the Romans, whom no sense
of past benefits could keep steady in friendship.   For
Maximilian, having made an advantageous peace with
France, with large compensation for past injuries, thought
he could do without England any longer ; or if he
hoped for anything more from that quarter, it would be
from England under a new master, such as Margaret
of Burgundy would give it.   Not that his desertion of
Henry was occasioned by any cordiality towards France,
for it is clear that Charles VIII. never trusted his friendship ; and having in 1494 married a sister of Ludovico
Sforza, he was easily drawn into the league of the
Italian powers against Charles in the following year.
This ought to have made him anxious once more to
cultivate amicable relations with Henry ; but instead of
doing this he continued his idle support of Perkin
Warbeck, persuaded, it would seem, that by this means
Henry could be easily driven out and a new sovereign
given to England, who would at once begin a war
with France.   And so sanguine was he in this matter
that he would not even listen to his brother-in-law,
Ludovico Sforza, who showed him that the opinion in
Spain as well as in Italy was that the league against

France would be greatly strengthened by Henry's adhesion.

But Henry was in no such danger as Maximilian
and the Yorkist refugees in Flanders fondly hoped. It
is an old mistake that he had any difficulty in ascer-
taining who Perkin really was, or troubled himself to
hunt out evidences of the murder of the princes.
The circumstances of the latter story were still shrouded
in darkness; but he had clearly informed Sir Gilbert
Talbot about Perkin's pedigree as early as July 1493.
Still, he could not obtain the delivery of the pretender, and he affected to take no notice of the
conspiracy; so that it really ripened and came to
maturity before he appeared to act at all.   But he
was none the less quite awake to all that was going
on.   "He chose," as Bacon says, "to work by counter-
mine."   Sir Robert Clifford and William Barley went
over to the Duchess Margaret as disaffected Yorkists,
and getting into the very heart of the conspiracy, revealed all the details, receiving a full pardon on their
return.   We must not, perhaps, be too sure of what
Bacon only mentions as "a strange tradition," that he
received secret intelligence even from the confessors and
chaplains of great men, and to give the better credit to
his own spies abroad, had them solemnly "cursed" (or
excommunicated) by their names at St. Paul's "amongst
the beadroll of the king's enemies."   But there is no
doubt the Yorkist intriguers were lulled into false
security, from which they were suddenly aroused by the
arrest of Lord Fitzwalter, Sir Simon Mountford, and
others, of whom the principal leaders were speedily sent
to the block.   Most appalling of all was the arrest and

execution of Sir William Stanley, Henry's own chamberlain, to whom he really owed his Crown, if not his life
at Bosworth. The degree of his complicity in the intrigue has never been ascertained. But it was essential
to show that treason in a trusted adviser was a far more
serious matter than treason in other persons; and a
certain family tie between him and the king (for his
brother, the Earl of Derby, had married Henry's mother,
the Countess of Richmond) perhaps only made his punishment a more imperious necessity.

The Duchess of Burgundy had really lost on Henry
VII.'s accession a considerable amount of property in
England, granted to her by the liberality of her brother,
Edward IV., and she exacted an engagement from her
pretended nephew that he would restore it as soon as he
had recovered the kingdom. The compact was witnessed
on the 10th of December 1494 by Sir Robert Clifford,
who immediately afterwards (about Christmas, Fabyan
tells us) returned to England, revealed the whole details
of the conspiracy, and impeached Sir William Stanley.
The arrests and executions which followed must have
considerably disconcerted a design which apparently was
just on the eve of execution. But in July following an
expedition for the invasion of England actually sailed ;
and a very pitiful affair it turned out to be—not for
want of aid from Maximilian, who seems to have been,
by his own account, at very serious expense to fit it out.
The fleet appeared off Deal, and a portion of Perkin's
followers disembarked, when the people of the district
rose in arms, killed and captured a good number of
them, and drove the rest back to their ships. Perkin
had no mind to land himself, but sailed away to try his

fortunes again in Ireland, where he had made such a favourable impression at the first.

Now, it might have been politic enough, from War-beck's own point of view, to betake himself to an island over which Henry had not yet succeeded in establishing his authority on anything like a secure basis. But it was a rather humiliating result of two years' preparation for the invasion of England that, after having a fleet equipped for him for the very purpose, the adventurer had not dared to set foot in the country himself. Maxi-milian, who had taken so great a part in fitting out the expedition, had been absurdly bragging to the Venetian ambassador that the Duke of York, as he called him, would very soon conquer England, and then, in fulfilment of the most solemn promises, turn his arms against the King of France. How he received the news of the un-successful attempt at Deal we are not informed; but even two months later he was still feeding himself with delusive hopes of the ultimate success of an enterprise which had made such an unpromising commencement. Very different was the view of a shrewd observer like Ferdinand, whose friendship for Henry, never more than lukewarm, being founded solely on considerations of policy, was carefully watching the turn of events for future guidance. To him the fiasco at Deal was pretty decisive —not so much of the pretensions of Perkin Warbeck, which he never seems to have credited, as of the utter impossibility of Henry's enemies dealing a serious blow at him with such a slender and ineffective weapon. "We now tell you," he wrote to his ambassador in England, "that as for the affair of him who calls himself duke, we hold it for a jest."

It was really little more even in the country to which
Warbeck had now withdrawn himself. For Ireland,
though still a considerable problem to Henry, was not
quite such a convenient playground for his enemies as
it had been at the beginning of his reign. How it became gradually more obedient to his rule we shall show
hereafter. Suffice it to say that at this time Kildare
was no longer Deputy. He had been attainted by an
Irish Parliament for disloyal conduct and sent prisoner
to England. The Earl of Desmond, however, was still
at large in Munster, and to him Perkin at once repaired.
Between them they laid siege to the loyal town of
Waterford—the only place in Ireland which had held
out for the king against Lambert Simnel,—Perkin's little
fleet blockading the harbour, while his Irish allies shut
in the town on the land side. The citizens, however,
discharged volleys of artillery against the ships, and in
eleven days Warbeck was compelled to raise the siege,
leaving more than one vessel in their hands. There
seems to have been nothing more left for him to do in
Ireland, and he accordingly proceeded to Scotland.

From the time of his first appearance as Duke of York
the Scots had been interested in his pretensions. He
had written to James IV. as he did to other sovereigns
for support, and apparently to him before others. James
had certainly assisted the expedition in which he made
his abortive attempt at Deal, and was reported at that
time to have sent ships and men to do him service.
For any enterprise against England the adventurer and
his pretensions offered an admirable pretext, and on his
arrival he was received by James with all the honour
due to a foreign prince. His wardrobe was plentifully

furnished at the expense of the Scottish king, and
messengers were despatched all over the kingdom with
letters of "wappin schawing" to array the lieges for
military service. But nearly a year seems to have elapsed
after his first arrival in Scotland before he actually crossed
the Border at the head of a small force in order to make
good his pretended right; and when he did so the
attempt was so utterly futile that it must have been a
complete disappointment, not only to the Scots but to
many who looked on from a distance, like the Venetian
agents in England, who seem to have been fully persuaded that Henry was in real dread of being driven
from his kingdom. It is not improbable that they
derived this impression from Henry himself, who doubtless had reasons of his own for magnifying to them the
difficulties by which he was surrounded.

It was in September 1496 that this invasion took
place. Henry, indeed, seems to have endeavoured to
avert it by negotiation, for he had that very month
commissioned Bishop Fox and others to treat for the
marriage of the Scotch king to his daughter Margaret.
But James apparently believed that by means of Perkin
he could recover Berwick from the English, and negotiate
under more favourable conditions. He had got together
a body of 1400 men of different nationalities, who
mustered at Ellam Kirk and crossed the Borders with
him and the pretender at their head. But there was
·nothing in the enterprise except the foreign element in
the invading army to distinguish it from any other
Border raid. There was a good deal of ravage and
burning and killing; but there was no sign whatever
that any English people were disposed to join the

invaders, and within three days the host had returned once more within Scottish territory. Perkin, it is said, was soon weary of the sight of cruelty and devastation committed by his Scotch allies, and begged King James to be a little more merciful to those whom he affected to call his subjects. Nothing, however, was so clear as that the alleged subjects cared very little for him who claimed their allegiance.

James is commonly represented as having been convinced by this experience that Perkin was an impostor. But whatever may have been his real opinion, he had pledged himself too deeply to Perkin's cause to admit that he had been imposed on. The pretender had actually during his stay in Scotland been allowed to take a wife from among the best blood of the Scotch nobility, and had in fact become related to James himself by his marriage with Katharine Gordon. Moreover, he still possessed value in the eyes of some sovereigns, for the French ambassador had been offering James 100,000 crowns if he would send him again into France. Not that Charles really believed in his pretensions, for he had not long before sent over to England a document, attested by his Council, showing that the young man's parentage was quite well known in France, and had offered to send over his father and mother for better evidence of the truth. But things had altered somewhat since then, for Henry had joined the league of European powers to keep the French out of Italy; and Charles conceived that, if he could but get hold of the young man again, he could still make use of him to keep the King of England in order.

James, however, had no notion of selling his guest

to any power, friendly or otherwise, and Warbeck remained under his protection for nearly another year.
But James most probably saw that he must come to an
arrangement with England in the long run, and did not
wish to be compelled to surrender him by treaty.   So
in July 1497 Warbeck with his wife embarked at Ayr,
with a small fleet under the command of the Scottish
captains, Andrew and Robert Barton; and he once
more bent his course to Ireland.   On the 26th of July
he landed at Cork, where he had been encouraged to
look for some support.   But Kildare, who had been re-
appointed as Deputy, was not willing immediately to
offend again; so he got little encouragement, and soon
determined to sail for Cornwall to escape being taken
prisoner.   The reasons which led him to direct his course
thither rather than elsewhere will appear hereafter, with
the sequel of his adventures.   But we must, in the first
place, deal with some other subjects.

CHAPTER VIII

IRELAND

Irish history is seldom or never more lucid than that of England; yet in a period of general obscurity we are not left without some light on the interesting question how it was that Ireland—the most difficult part of his dominions to pacify—became comparatively tractable under Henry VII. If other rulers before and after him have found the Irish problem present difficulties almost insuperable, to him very soon after his accession those difficulties were as formidable as they could possibly be. The rebellion in favour of Lambert Simnel had been like a spontaneous movement of almost the whole country. It had been supported by the Lord Deputy, with the principal bishops, abbots, and nobles, and almost all the judges; and even after it was put down, the idea of punishing those who took part in it was wholly out of the question. In fact, as we have seen, Henry was obliged to proclaim a general amnesty, and to admit even the greatest offenders into favour with but slender guarantees for their future loyalty. Yet Perkin Warbeck met with distinctly less support than Simnel had done, especially on his second and third visits to the country; and during the remainder of the reign the Irish, though they had wars among themselves, never became a serious danger to the peace of England.

For some time before Henry came to the throne the Kings of England had been accustomed to appoint a Viceroy or Lord Lieutenant of Ireland, commonly a member of the royal family, who never visited the island, and under him a Lord Deputy, on whom the practical work of government naturally fell. Following the established practice, Henry, within six months after his accession, appointed his uncle Jasper, Duke of Bedford, Lord Lieutenant. As to the deputy ship he tried, as we have seen, to negotiate with the Earl of Kildare that he should be Deputy for a term of years, on condition that he should come over to England and bring with him an account of the revenues of Ireland, out of which he should have a salary of £1000 a year if they could sustain the charge. Kildare of course never came, and he and all Ireland supported Lambert Simnel. Sir Richard Edgecombe next year took what slender securities he could for the behaviour of him and others, and Kildare was reinstated as Lord Deputy. Yet scarcely had Sir Richard sailed for England when complaints began to be made against Kildare by the Archbishop of Armagh, an Italian, who claimed to be the only man in Ireland who had openly opposed Simnel's coronation, and begged that, if Kildare retained the rule, he might be appointed Chancellor to keep him in check.

Henry, however, had a way of his own of bringing the Irish to repentance for their rebellion. Just after the battle of Stoke he sent for Kildare and the other Irish lords who had been taken prisoners fighting in

behalf of the pretender, and they appeared together
before the Council. He had a long talk with them
about their rebellion, in the end of which he said to
them, " My masters of Ireland, you will crown apes at
length ! " They were then dismissed from their ex- ·
amination, and being led away in procession, were not
a little comforted to perceive that the face of the axe
which was borne before them was turned away from
them—a sign that their lives were spared. Nor was
this all. They were ordered to dine that day in Court,
where Lambert Simnel waited upon them in the character
of cupbearer. This was the most galling indignity to
which they could have been exposed. " None would
have taken the cup out of his hands," says a lively Irish
writer of the next generation, " but bade the great
Devil of Hell him take before that ever they saw him."
Only one man of the company felt quite at ease— the
Lord of Howth, who had sent the king privy notice of
all that was done in Ireland, and enabled him the better
to meet the rebels in England. " Bring me the cup,"
he said, " if the wine be good, and I shall drink it off
for the wine's sake and mine own sake also. And as for
thee," he added, addressing Simnel, " as thou art, so I
leave thee, a poor innocent."

After Sir Richard Edgecombe's visit to Ireland no
notice appears to have been taken of any complaints
against Kildare for about two years ; but on the 28th
of July 1490 the king felt it necessary to write to him,
requiring his presence in England. Whether Warbeck
had by that time made his first appearance in Ireland is
uncertain—he is commonly supposed to have landed there
in 1491. All that was formally objected to the earl on

this occasion was a breach of the statutes against giving
liveries and keeping retinues. Nor was it the king's
intention to treat offences like these with severity ; for a
pardon was sent to him for mere illegalities of this sort
on condition that he would present himself before the
king within ten months. But Kildare was not accustomed to a summons, and was not more ready to come
over than when he received the more gentle invitation
sent by John Estrete. He simply allowed the ten months
to expire, and then got the Irish Council to write in his
behalf that, in consequence of the state of the country,
his presence in Ireland was absolutely indispensable.
The letter also assured the king that he was as faithful
in his allegiance as any subject could be ; and it was
signed by fifteen members of the Council, the Archbishop
of Armagh being one. The earl at the same time wrote
a letter of his own, giving as the special cause of his
detention that he had been called in to settle a dispute
between his cousin, the Earl of Desmond, and Lord Bourke
of Connaught ; and he suggested that if the king would
send over to Ireland some trusty servant, he would get
all the lords, spiritual and temporal, of Munster, and the
Lord Bourke and all the lords of Connaught, to be bound
to his Majesty like himself, and many whose ancestors
had never been bound to any King of England would be
compelled to acknowledge Henry as their sovereign.
Finally, the Earl of Desmond and three other lords wrote,
at his instigation, from Limerick that they had persuaded
him to remain in Ireland, not merely on account of the
dispute between Desmond and Bourke, but also for fear
the north should be destroyed in his absence by Irish
enemies recently subdued, and likewise in consideration

of the dangers that might befall his valuable person at sea both going and returning.

What Henry thought of these excuses we may pretty well imagine. But as Kildare's influence was paramount, he could not be hastily removed; and he remained as Deputy one year longer. In the spring of 1492, how-ever, the king having by that time fully satisfied himself of the fact that he had given underhand support to Perkin Warbeck—"the French lad," as the earl called him, writing to Henry to disavow it—at length dismissed him from that office and appointed Walter Fitzsimons, Archbishop of Dublin, in his room. The whole government of Ireland at the same time changed hands. Kildare's father-in-law, Baron Portlester, was deprived of the offices of Lord Chancellor and Lord Treasurer, which he held together, the former being conferred on Alexander Plunket and the latter upon James Ormond, soon afterwards knighted for his services to the king, a bastard son of the fifth Earl of Ormond. The long reign of the Geraldines in Ireland, who by favour of the House of York had borne sway for nearly forty years, was at length interrupted for a time.

The rival house of the Butlers was not at this time violently opposed to the Fitzgeralds. Its head was Thomas, seventh Earl of Ormond, who lived in England and was chamberlain to Henry's queen. His cousin, Piers Butler, who afterwards succeeded to the title, managed his estates in Ireland as his deputy. But when James Ormond was sent over to Ireland as Lord Treasurer he appears also to have received a commission from the earl to act as his "general and special attorney" in Kilkenny. There soon arose a conflict between his

authority and that of Piers Butler. Kildare had taken
the side of the latter and given him his daughter in
marriage. But Sir James Ormond, now that Kildare
was in disgrace, not only took possession of the Earl of
Ormond's lands, but was recognised by the Irish, who
cared little about legitimacy of birth, as Earl of Ormond
himself. Even some old Irish historians speak of him
by that title. The quarrel between him and Kildare
grew warm. He marched up to Dublin, and a regular
faction fight took place in the streets, in the course of
which some houses were set on fire, and he was pursued
by Kildare himself into the chapter-house of St. Patrick's
Church, where he barred himself in and would trust no
assurance of his safety till, a hole being cut in the door,
as he feared to put his hand through to shake hands
with the earl, the latter put in his to shake hands with
him.

Soon after this Viscount Gormanston was made
Deputy in place of the Archbishop of Dublin, who went
over to England to report the state of the country to
the king himself, and was immediately followed by
Kildare, anxious to justify himself against a multitude
of accusations. The way in which he did so has been
told with a considerable spice of Irish humour by one of
the compilers of *The Book of Howth.* The Bishop of
Meath, whom he had arrested in a church into which he
had pursued him with drawn sword, was his principal
accuser, and charged him with a number of misdemeanours. He replied that he could make no answer
for lack of learned counsel. The king desired him to
choose any counsel in England, and he should have time
to instruct him. "Then," said the earl, "I shall make

answer to-morrow; but I doubt I shall not have that good fellow that I would choose." "By my truth thou shalt," replied the king. "Give me your hand," said the earl, with a freedom altogether ignorant of Court manners. "Here it is," replied Henry, amused at the *naïveté* of his demeanour. The earl in fact treated the king quite on equal terms, addressing him with the familiar "thou," as he did also several members of the Council, who seeing the king's disposition, took the matter in good part also. "Well," said the king to him, "when will you choose your counsel?" "Never, if he be put to his choice," interposed the bishop. "Thou liest, bald bishop," replied the earl, "as soon as thou wouldest choose a fair wench if thou hadst thy wish"; and turning to the king, declared he had three stories to tell against his accuser. "Well," said the king, "you had better make a careful choice as to your counsel, for I think he will have enough to do for you." "Shall I choose now?" said the earl. "If you think good," replied Henry. "Well," said the earl, "I can see no better man than you, and by St. Bride I will choose none other." "A wiser man might have chosen worse," said the king, laughing.

"You see the sort of man he is," said the bishop at length; "all Ireland cannot rule him." "No?" said the king, "then he must be the man to rule all Ireland"; and accordingly, the writer adds, the king made him Deputy again, and sent him back to Ireland with great gifts. But the narrative certainly runs on a little too fast in that matter; for it was not till after about four years had elapsed that the king ventured again on the experiment of placing Ireland under Kildare's government. Meanwhile he proposed to make the whole administration of the country English and directly responsible to himself. Having now two sons he, on the 12th of September 1494, created the second, Henry, Lord Lieutenant in place of his uncle, Jasper, Duke of Bedford, and under him he appointed Sir Edward Poynings as Deputy, the experienced commander of the troops sent to besiege Sluys two years before. Henry Dean, Bishop-elect of Bangor, was at the same time made Chancellor of Ireland, Thomas Butler, Master of the Rolls, and Sir Hugh Conway, Treasurer.

The king evidently hoped to steer clear of Irish factions and administer justice in the country with strict impartiality, and if any man could give effect to his wishes in this matter it was Poynings. He entered on his office with one apparent advantage. The two rivals, Kildare and Ormond, both consented to act under him ; and with them he set out on an expedition to Ulster against O'Donnell, who was in league with the Scots. But not to be influenced in some degree by Irish faction on one side or the other was a sheer impossibility. When they reached O'Hanlon's country (in Armagh) Sir James Ormond accused Kildare not only of intriguing against the Deputy by sending men to assist O'Hanlon, but of inciting the Irish to murder him. News also arrived that Lord James Fitzgerald, the earl's brother, had seized the king's castle of Carlow and set upon it the standard and cognisance of the Geraldines. The Ulster expedition was abandoned, and Poynings marched southwards to recover Carlow, which he only succeeded in doing after a lengthened siege. He then proceeded to Drogheda, where he held a Parliament, perhaps the most memorable that was ever held in Ireland, as certainly no other Parliament in that country made laws which endured so long as two which were then enacted, and were known for centuries afterwards as the "Poynings Acts."

By the first of these it was ordained that no Parliament should be held in Ireland in future until the king's Council in England had approved not only of its being summoned, but also of the Acts which the Lieutenant and Council of Ireland proposed to pass in it. By the second the laws enacted before that time in England were extended to Ireland also. Thus the Irish legislature was made entirely dependent upon England. The Irish Parliament had no power to originate anything, but was only free to accept or (if they were very bold) to reject measures drawn up by the Irish Council and approved already by the king and his Council in England before they were submitted to discussion. Little as this looks like parliamentary government, such was the state of subjection in which the Irish Parliament remained by virtue of this law for nearly three centuries later. Almost the whole time, that is to say, that Ireland had a separate Parliament at all it remained in this manner restricted in its action by the legislation of Sir Edward Poynings; for, however inconsistent such a state might be with the development of constitutional principles, no better means could be devised of keeping the Irish legislature in harmony with the Government of England.

It should be remembered, however, that Henry VII. merely sought to do in Ireland what there is every reason to suppose he practically did in England. Legislation was not at this time considered to be the chief business of a

Parliament. The responsibility of framing new laws and
ordinances lay chiefly, or it may be said entirely, with
the king's Council; and in the following reign we have
in some cases the first drafts of laws actually passed
in the English Parliament, and of petitions supposed to
have originated in the Commons, drawn up in the hand-
writing of the king's ministers. It was upon the king's
business, not upon the nation's, that Parliament was
understood to be called together; and if his Majesty did
not make too great demands upon them for money there
were few in either House—especially in the Commons—
likely to dispute the wisdom of measures which the
Council had thought expedient to be passed for the public
weal.

Besides these two specially memorable Acts, there
were also several other measures passed in this Parliament
at Drogheda with practically the same end in view—the
establishment of a system of English government with
direct responsibility to the king in England. There
were enactments conceived in a very just spirit to keep
down faction, to suppress party war-cries, and to punish
the practices of coyne and livery. Thus oppression and
feudalism within the land were counteracted as far as
Parliament could do so. But the great matter was to
secure that English rule should be really enforced, and
that all who held important offices should be made responsible to the central government. Kildare was attainted, as a matter of course. It was also ordained that
the principal castles throughout Ireland should always
be under the command of Englishmen. But a very
significant statute was also passed to annul what was
declared to be " an usurpation or pretended prescription,"

K

by which Ireland was supposed to be an asylum for
English rebels, who were received and harboured there
in defiance of the king's writs sent out of England.
This theory had gained strength under the weak rule of
Henry VI., when Richard, Duke of York—regarded as a
rebel in England—held undisputed authority in Ireland;
and the mischief resulting from it had been sufficiently
apparent in the support that had been given of late to
"these two lads," as the Act called them, meaning Simnel
and Warbeck.

Legislation, however, could do little to enlarge the
sphere of English authority, which was scarcely recognised beyond the pale; and it lay with the inhabitants
of four counties—Dublin, Meath, Kildare, and Louth—
to protect their borders against inroads of the wild Irish.
This duty Poynings strongly enforced; but he likewise
did his utmost to extend the king's authority beyond
these limits.   He came to an understanding with
M'Murrough, O'Brien, O'Neil, and other chieftains,
mainly, if not entirely, through pensions given them to
aid against other enemies; but even he was not the man
to "rule all Ireland."   He who could make the nearest
approach to that feat was Kildare, whom he had sent
over to England as a traitor, and whose kinsmen gave
quite as much trouble in his absence, or probably rather
more, than if he had been in Ireland.

But Kildare, before a year had passed, either justified himself to Henry's satisfaction or succeeded in con-
vincing him that he would be really less dangerous in
Ireland as Deputy than in the Tower of London as a
prisoner.   During his imprisonment Perkin Warbeck
paid his second visit to Ireland after his failure to land

in Kent, and was supported by Kildare's cousin, the Earl
of Desmond. Other Geraldines also gave a good deal of
trouble in the earl's absence. Poynings returned from
Ireland early in 1496, and some time afterwards Kildare
was allowed to go back as Deputy, leaving his son Gerald
as a hostage with the king. He remained in authority
till the end of the reign of Henry VII., and even for
many years after. In 1503 he was summoned to England, where he remained three months, and was allowed
to take back his son. The king had been apparently
satisfied with his conduct in the meanwhile; and the
friendly personal feeling that had grown up between
him and the earl served greatly to mitigate, if not
altogether to remove, the Irish difficulty in Henry's days.
The earl at least was out and out the most powerful man
on the eastern side of the country, and in 1504 he
obtained a great victory, with a much inferior force,
over a confederation of clans in the west at the battle of
Knocktoe, and thus advanced the king's authority in a
region where it was apt to be little regarded.

It need hardly be said that it was not at his instigation that Warbeck came to Ireland for the last time in
1497, a year after he had been restored as Deputy. It
was at the solicitation of Sir James Ormond, who, pre-
ferring to be recognised by the Butlers as Earl of Ormond,
and exercise among them an undisputed authority rather
than to do his duty either to his kinsman or his prince,
had twice refused obedience to the king's letters summon-
ing him to England, and had thrown off all pretence of
loyalty. He was killed that same year in an encounter
with Sir Piers Butler.

CHAPTER IX

FROM the very beginning of his reign Henry had been
anxious to cultivate friendly relations with all foreign
powers, and to fortify himself with valuable alliances
abroad. But what could have been the value of an
English alliance at that time to any considerable State?
England had lost her old possessions in France, her
throne was insecure, and whatever force she possessed
was more in danger of being wasted in renewed civil
jars than likely to bring any accession of strength to an
ally. No European sovereign, in truth, was likely to
offer very high terms for so precarious an advantage.
Yet the state of England itself was a matter of concern
to other nations, and the character of its ruler was
scarcely of less importance. France had helped to set
Henry on the throne, doubtless in the belief that a
Lancastrian prince who owed so much to her protection
and favour was more likely than the Yorkist usurper
Richard to leave her undisturbed. Spain, on the other
hand, was more anxious to appeal to the national senti-
ments of Englishmen and form a strong alliance against
France, without paying too dearly for the privilege.

We have seen already how this policy was followed

out by Ferdinand and Isabella. Henry, however, took
no notice of their bad faith, for which there was only this
excuse, that, being then engaged in their final struggle
with the Moors, they had scarcely the means of carrying
on at the same time a war with France. The conquest of Granada was in itself a far greater object than
the restoration of Roussillon and Cerdagne, although
these districts undoubtedly were a source of danger to
Spain as long as they remained in the hands of a foreign
power. It was achieved in the beginning of 1492, the
very year in which Henry invaded France. The fame of
it rang through Christendom, nor was England sparing of
her congratulations on an event so long unprecedented as
the gaining of fresh territory from the infidels. A rich
and important kingdom which had been in possession of
the Moors for over seven hundred years had been added
not only to the dominions of Ferdinand and Isabella,
but to the Christian world ; and Cardinal Morton invited
a large assembly at St. Paul's to celebrate the achievement.

The dual monarchy of Spain was greatly strengthened,
but, instead of preparing for a war with France, the
Spanish sovereigns endeavoured to procure the cession
of Roussillon and Cerdagne by negotiation, leaving
Henry and Maximilian to do the fighting for them.
Maximilian did nothing, Henry, with a very slight degree
of fighting, obtained his own terms from the enemy,
and shortly afterwards Ferdinand and Isabella made their
peace with France also. But in this treaty—the treaty
of Barcelona, as it was called (19th January 1493)—
having obtained the much-desired cession of Roussillon
and Cerdagne, they agreed, in violation of all their
pledges to Henry, to aid France against all enemies,

especially the English, and not to marry any of their
children with the royal family of England without the
express consent of the French king. Henry at that
time sent an ambassador to Spain, who came to them at
Barcelona and evidently made some very inconvenient
inquiries; but they simply answered that they were
going to send an embassy of their own to England.
They were *going* to send, but they certainly did not
feel any necessity for haste, and what first prompted
them to redeem their promise seems to have been the
complaints of Spanish merchants in England that they
were subjected to new restrictions. To remonstrate
upon this subject they were about to have despatched
in November 1494 an envoy named Sasiola; but he was
taken ill, and his illness was made a very good excuse
for a delay of two whole years after the treaty of Barcelona, when they at length sent to England—not a
very splendid embassy, but an agent of whom Henry
VII. had already had some experience—Dr. de Puebla.

Henry was rather surprised at his appointment. The
man was neither of noble birth, nor of high personal
character, nor even of a dignified presence, for he was a
cripple. He was a mere pettifogging lawyer, who no
doubt had shown himself very useful to the Spanish
sovereigns in negotiating the hard conditions from which
Henry was now emancipated. But if Ferdinand thought
him a sufficiently good representative of Spanish interests
in England, Henry had no reason to object. He had
taken the measure of the man, and also of Ferdinand.
In the course of a few years complaints were heard from
Spaniards that De Puebla served England far better
than his own country; and though Ferdinand did not

see fit to recall him, he more than once expressed vexation at the fact that his ambassador had given Henry some undue advantage. De Puebla, in fact, somehow or other became a very great advocate of English interests and of English views in almost everything. Although a man who gave satisfaction to no one else, but excited unpleasantness in every one with whom he came in contact, he always got on very well with Henry, and Henry got on very well with him. Henry took him freely into counsel, showed him all the difficulties by which he was surrounded, expressed the most complete devotion to the interests of Spain, and finally inspired him with a profound conviction that he knew all the secrets of the King of England's heart. The doctor, indeed, was to some extent dependent on Henry's splendid hospitality : for England was a dear country to live in, and De Puebla was not the only ambassador in those days who found great difficulties in keeping up appearances on the scanty and irregular remittances he received from his own Court. He dined for months together at the palace, and once when he was observed making his way to Court, Henry, having asked for what purpose he could be coming, laughed not a little when the courtiers replied, "To eat." The queen indeed, and her mother also, would sometimes inquire whether his masters in Spain did not provide him with sufficient food.

It was early in the year 1495 that De Puebla came on this his second mission to England. He met with a cordial reception, and having excused the delay of the embassy which Ferdinand and Isabella had promised to send, unfolded the causes of his mission, the main object of which was certainly not merely to represent the grievances of Spanish merchants. A great change had taken place in Ferdinand's relations with France, and De Puebla desired Henry, as a Christian prince, to aid the Pope against Charles VIII., then in Italy. His sovereigns also regretted that relations had become considerably strained between Henry and Maximilian, King of the Romans, on account of certain conspiracies fostered by the latter in England (those, namely, in favour of Perkin Warbeck); and if Henry would make use of their good offices they would be glad to promote a reconciliation. Henry's answer was in the best spirit. He accepted the excuses for the delay of the embassy, although, as he significantly wrote to Ferdinand and Isabella, he had been otherwise informed as to the causes of it. He could not believe the Pope to be in real danger, otherwise his Holiness, desiring aid from England, would surely have had the civility to write to himself. As to the King of the Romans, though he had given him not the slightest pretext for quarrelling with him, and had done more for him than any other prince, he was quite willing to forgive his ingratitude and accept the good offices of Ferdinand and Isabella, if Maximilian himself was willing to be reconciled to him.

The fact is that, although it was but two years since Ferdinand and Isabella had abandoned England and made a secret league with France against her, they were now most anxious to reverse what they had done, and to gain England's adhesion to a new league which they were busy forming against France. The success of Charles VIII.'s invasion of Italy had completely changed the aspect of affairs, rousing the jealousy of his more powerful neighbours, while his imprudence had alienated the friends who had invoked his assistance in Italy itself. But this was a matter that Henry could afford to treat with philosophic calmness. He ·did not, indeed, wish to see France too powerful, but his continental neighbours were much more concerned than himself to prevent such a result, and he had no desire to go to war again merely for their benefit. The league, indeed, was actually made without him at Venice on the 31st of March '495, the parties to it being Pope Alexander VI., Maximilian, Ferdinand and Isabella, Venice and Milan. But Ferdinand and Isabella, after it was concluded, used every effort to convince Henry that it was for his interest that he too should join it. They could not, indeed, but admit that Maximilian had given him serious grounds of complaint, and moreover that he was under no particular obligations even to themselves, but was free to make what alliances he pleased. But they urged him to consider that France was not to be depended on, and though the old treaties between England and Spain had now lapsed, they were willing to renew the project of a marriage between Prince Arthur and Katharine on the conditions formerly agreed to. Besides, the league would be one of mutual defence, and Henry would be benefited by it if either France or the so-called Duke of York made war against him.

It was clear that the alliance of England with France at this time would have been a very serious danger to the Holy League, and Ferdinand wrote to De Puebla to do everything in his power to interrupt it. France, on the other hand, was not less alive to the great importance of England's continued friendship, and was making some new and very advantageous offers for a stricter

alliance, to be cemented by the marriage of Prince Arthur
to a daughter of the Duke of Bourbon. Even if Henry
meant only to be neutral, France would be willing in
some way to recompense his neutrality, whereas if he
cordially took part with her, the French king could probably induce James IV. not to favour Perkin Warbeck
or molest the English Border. These things Henry did
not hesitate to suggest to the Spanish ambassador. But
he had a still stronger argument against joining the
Holy League, which it was really difficult to answer.
How could he be asked to enter such a league while
Maximilian was giving manifest aid and support to
Perkin Warbeck? So long as the King of the Romans
pursued such a policy he acted as Henry's enemy, and
his alliance with England could be but a dissembled
friendship. Nay, the alliance he had actually made
with Ferdinand only gave him greater power to do
Henry an ill turn; for it was cemented by two marriages
which were at this time arranged and soon took effect—
the first between the Archduke Philip, son of Maximilian, and Joanna, second daughter of Ferdinand and
Isabella, an elder sister of Katharine of Arragon; and
the second between Prince John, the son and heir-
apparent of the Spanish sovereigns, and Maximilian's
daughter Margaret. How could Henry marry his son
to Katharine if her sister was to marry Philip, who with
his father, Maximilian, had been giving not only an
asylum to Warbeck, but active assistance to an expedition against England? Ferdinand really had more need
of England at this time than England had of him. He
insisted that he could easily persuade Maximilian to
abandon Warbeck,—nay, that he had positive assurance

of Maximilian's desire to abandon him and be reconciled to Henry ; and after Warbeck had actually left Flanders without having succeeded in landing in England, his pretensions had become so contemptible that there was no fear, Ferdinand pleaded, of Maximilian abetting them again. The Kings of France and Scotland no doubt might—in fact most probably would ; and that was all the greater reason for Henry now joining the league. But a Scotch embassy had just arrived in Spain, and Ferdinand believed he would be able, if Henry favoured his wishes, to prevent the King of Scots befriending Warbeck. In short, Ferdinand would do anything and everything to get Henry to desert France and join the Holy League. He was even ready, if all else failed, to become security to Henry for the strict fulfilment by Maximilian of a clause by which he would have been bound, not merely to refrain from aiding Warbeck, but actually to aid Henry against him. But De Puebla wisely refrained from communicating this offer to the king, and was afterwards thanked by Ferdinand for his exercise of a discretion which was no doubt allowed to him by his instructions.

It was, indeed, a difficult matter to answer for Maximilian. No sooner was one assurance framed for Henry's acceptance than it was falsified by the sailing of the expedition with which Warbeck attempted to invade England. Ferdinand had hoped that his own and the Duke of Milan's exhortations would have availed to induce the King of the Romans to withdraw his countenance from the pretender ; for Maximilian had married only the year before Bianca Maria Sforza, niece of the new Duke Ludovico, by whose exhortations mainly he

had been drawn into the league. But the policy of
Maximilian and the Archduke Philip was for the present
governed by Margaret of Burgundy, and no arguments
of friends, relations, or allies could induce them to desert
the pretender until the experiment to which they had
committed themselves had turned out to be an unequivocal
failure. And this was not the conclusion they came to
from his ill success at Deal ; for, as they were doubtless
well aware from the first, if attacking England failed,
he had still a chance in Ireland, and a still better one
in Scotland. And though Warbeck lost the first two
chances with amazing rapidity, he was royally received
in Scotland within little more than four months after
his attempt at Deal. Maximilian just so far yielded to
the pressure put upon him as to agree to the inclusion
of England in the league, but he must have some proviso
inserted relative to " the Duke of York," whose cause
he could not bring himself altogether to abandon.

It is needless to say that Henry would not listen to a
proposal which in any way recognised the adventurer's
pretensions ; and Maximilian's envoy, having gone as far
as his instructions warranted, desired him to send Lord
Egremont—an able diplomatist, probably of the Percy
family (though our peerage historians know nothing of
him), who had been employed before this in negotiations
with Scotland—to the Court of Maximilian, then staying
at Nordlingen in Suabia. He arrived at the beginning of
January 1496. But the political situation had changed
not a little since Perkin left the Netherlands, and his
first inquiry was whether the league, which his master
had been asked to join, was not virtually dissolved. For
in fact a separate peace had been made with France by

Ludovico Sforza more than two months before, and there were rumours that Venice, as well as Milan, was included in the treaty.

The truth was that Charles VIII., even after winning the decisive battle of Fornovo, could not immediately make his way out of Italy without leaving in the lurch his cousin Louis, Duke of Orleans, who was closely besieged in Novara by Ludovico Sforza. Louis was the grandson of that former Duke of Orleans, brother of Charles VI., who was murdered in the streets of Paris, by his marriage with Valentine, daughter of Gian Galeazzo, first Duke of Milan. He had thus a claim on the duchy, for the Sforzas were not legitimate successors; and unfortunately for himself, he had shown that he intended to make good his right. He had seized Novara, but was surrounded by the forces of Ludovico. He and his soldiers suffered extreme privations, and Charles called in Swiss mercenaries to raise the siege. But Ludovico was willing to make terms if the French would but leave Italy and engage to respect his rights in future. A treaty was accordingly made in which his claims were fully satisfied, and he undertook to give the French king every assistance to maintain his hold on Naples. The Venetians were strongly urged to give in their adhesion to this treaty, but they refused. Ludovico Sforza had acted in the matter with singular duplicity. He still professed to adhere to the Holy League, while he had in fact pledged himself to facilitate what that league was founded to prevent—another French invasion of Italy. The allies, however, seem to have persuaded themselves that his agreement with France was only a matter of temporary convenience, and that it was better for their

interests not to cast him off. So Maximilian, after con-
sulting the representatives of the league at his Court,
assured Lord Egremont in the first place that Venice had
made no peace whatever with France, and secondly, that
in the treaty made by the Duke of Milan there was an
express clause stating that he still remained a member
of the league. So all was made smooth for the King
of England's entrance into the league also ; but it was
owing to the ambassadors at Maximilian's Court that the
result was not quite the reverse. For Maximilian him- .
self had drawn up a reply to Lord Egremont in which
he justified his conduct with regard to Perkin Warbeck,
firmly believing him, he said, to be the real son of
Edward IV., but offered, if Henry would join the league,
to negotiate a ten years' truce between him and the
pretender; insisting also that the King of England
should be bound to invade France at Easter. This,
however, was suppressed in consequence of the united
remonstrances of the Spanish, the Venetian, the Neapoli-
tan, and the Milanese ambassadors, who unanimously insisted that any allusion to the so-called " Duke of York "
would be fatal to the negotiation, and that it would be
very advisable that Maximilian should now drop him
altogether; moreover, that the King of England had
distinctly refused to be bound to act on the offensive
lest he should be made a cat's-paw, but that, if admitted
unconditionally, the Spanish sovereigns would pledge
themselves on his behalf that he would do his part along
with the other confederates. The ambassadors further
added that if they failed to secure England as an ally,
she would certainly unite with France and so become
their enemy.

Maximilian was uncomfortable. He had done so much to help Perkin Warbeck's enterprise, and he had still hopes that it would be successful; yet he was to make an ally of Henry VII., who, he was sure, would not go to war with France, whereas "the Duke of York" would certainly do so if he only obtained the Crown! He could not help thinking, in his own wise head, that the other powers were wrong; that Henry VII. could do the league neither good nor evil, and that it was only from his fear of the favour they might show to "the Duke of York" that he was anxious to be on good terms with himself and the league or with France. He, however, yielded to the representations of his allies, and sent to the Spanish ambassador in England—because he thought he could not do it himself, considering his engagements to Perkin Warbeck—ample instructions for receiving Henry into the league on his undertaking to attack France. This again was a condition by which Henry had already refused to be bound. It would have been no doubt an immense advantage to the league if Henry had diverted the attention of Charles from Italy by an invasion of France. But former experience had warned him that he was likely, if he entered into any engagements with such allies, to have the whole burden of the war thrown upon himself; and he doubted particularly whether Maximilian would be ready to begin the attack along with him. It was enough for him, however, from a diplomatic point of view, that Maximilian was now visibly yielding. He sent his old friend Christopher Urswick to the emperor at Augsburg; who, after giving him a hearing, was persuaded by the ambassadors of the other powers to agree with him for the admission of Henry into the league—if possible with the obligation to attack France, but if this was refused, on the same terms as the other confederates.

Maximilian, there can be little doubt, believed it would be worth Henry's while to buy his friendship. Ferdinand and Isabella, on the contrary, had been in serious anxiety lest, instead of joining the league at all, he should ally himself with France and marry Arthur to the Duke of Bourbon's daughter. Great therefore was their relief when they were informed by Henry himself that he had dismissed a French embassy, requiring Charles to evacuate Naples, restore Ostia to the Pope, and forbear to disturb the peace of Europe. They had reason to believe that Henry told the truth, and they were not mistaken. He had, indeed, at one time thought of requiring the league to be reconstructed in England, rather than that he should be simply admitted into it as a new confederate ; and as De Puebla had power to act not only for his own sovereigns but also for the Pope and Maximilian, it might not have been difficult to do so. But considering the urgency of Ferdinand and Isabella, and the fact that the French were even then preparing to invade Italy a second time, Henry sent Robert Sherbourne, afterwards Bishop of Chichester, to Rome to declare his entry into the league, with an exemption, which was allowed to him, from certain specific obligations incumbent on the other allies. This was done upon the 18th of July 1496.

The news was hailed with delight by all the other confederates, except by Maximilian, who was still keeping up communications with the young man in Scotland. Henry's accession practically made it a new league altogether, which was proclaimed at Venice, and celebrated by the burning of bonfires and ringing of bells for three successive days. The Pope, in acknowledgment of this timely aid, sent him a sword and cap of maintenance, which were received with due reverence on All Saints' day, and a solemn procession took place at St. Paul's in honour of the event. Isabella too, though she could have wished to bind Henry to make war on France at once, expressed great satisfaction at the event, and was now particularly anxious that the marriage of Arthur and Katharine should be pressed on, as some guarantee for the permanence of the alliance. For though it was a great gain to have won Henry over to the league on any terms, the conditions were not satisfactory, and if he could not make war on France at once, he must at least be bound to assist Spanish vessels at sea, and De Puebla, as he saw opportunity, must urge him to still further concessions. For if he did no more than make preparations for war, the longer he did so the greater would be the offers made to him by France. He must be warned that the French king was still intent on making himself lord of Italy, that he had already a hold on Milan and Genoa, and that if he were allowed to keep these places no other power would be able to resist him. The Pope himself would become merely his chaplain. Henry really ought to rescue the patrimony of St. Peter from spoliation, and even in kindness to the King of France himself, prevent him rushing to his own destruction.

Such were the views of Isabella of Castile, as communicated confidentially to her ambassador. But she and her husband were not unmindful of certain pledges

they had given to Henry in order to induce him to enter
the league at all.   Henry must be effectually protected
from molestation on the side of Scotland.   They would
endeavour to make James give up his patronage of Perkin
Warbeck and be friends with Henry.   Some years
before they had, for purposes of their own, dangled
before the eyes of the Scotch king the hope of obtaining
one of their daughters in marriage, without any serious
intention of fulfilling his expectation.   But now James
had sent an ambassador to them repeating the request
and stating that, as he had some grounds of dissatisfac-
tion with France, he would gladly ally himself politically
with Spain instead.   The Spanish sovereigns were a little
perplexed.   They would now really have been willing
apparently to marry one daughter to the Prince of Wales
and one to the King of Scotland, if they had daughters
to spare, as it would have tended to the more complete
isolation of France and to promote a friendly understanding between England and Scotland.   But they had
already other projects for all their four daughters.   So
they determined to keep the renewed negotiations for
Arthur's marriage with Katharine a profound secret,
amuse the King of Scots with the project as long as
possible, and in the meantime urge Henry to give James
one of his own daughters instead, with a suitable dowry.

With this view they sent into Scotland Don Pedro
de Ayala, a negotiator of a very different stamp from
De Puebla in England.   His suavity of manners and
perfect knowledge of the world rendered him the fittest
man possible to smooth down whatever was rough in the
difficult business of diplomacy.   His sovereigns greatly
regretted that he arrived in Scotland too late to prevent

James's invasion of England in favour of Perkin Warbeck.
But from the moment of his arrival there things tended
gradually towards peace.   He soon acquired great influence over James, who had a very high regard for him,
and of whose character and accomplishments he wrote a
very interesting account for the benefit of Ferdinand
and Isabella.   While residing in England a little later
he was described by careful and dispassionate observers
as the only man there that really understood Scotland.
The English, as a rule, flew in a passion whenever Scotland or Scotchmen were spoken about.   How, in the
face of prejudices so general, Henry ventured at last to
give his daughter to the Scotch king is only a little less
wonderful than how Ayala should have mitigated Scotch
prejudices on the other side and got James to give up
his demand for a Spanish princess for the prospect of an
English one.

On this subject we shall have more to say hereafter.
For the present a few words are necessary as to Henry's
relations with other princes.   Even before he had joined
the league a resumption of commercial intercourse with
Flanders had been found absolutely necessary on both
sides ; and Philip, having sent over to England ambassadors of the highest standing in his country, a mercantile treaty, called the *Intercursus Magnus*, was concluded
between him and Henry on the 24th of February 1496.
This in itself no doubt exerted a considerable influence
on Maximilian, who was so slowly brought to the disagreeable conviction that all his efforts and expense on
behalf of Perkin Warbeck had been utterly thrown
away.   Henry saw his way was safe, rejected the offers
of France, and entered the league in July following ; so

that in the latter part of the year France found herself
completely surrounded by a circle of confederates pledged
to keep her thenceforth out of Italy. Charles was
obliged to sign a treaty for the evacuation of Naples,
where he had still some garrisons after he had left Italy
with his army, and somewhat later to make a truce
with Ferdinand, whose armies, now having possession
of Roussillon, harassed his southern frontier. This was
meant to pave the way for a general peace, and Ferdinand did not forget to include England in particular in
the truce, his other allies having done little, after the
danger was past, to relieve him from the burden of an
expensive war.

So French ambition had been muzzled for the time,
and the peace of Europe seemed tolerably secure, when
the sudden death of Charles VIII. gave rise to new com
binations, of which we shall speak hereafter.

CHAPTER X

DOMESTIC HISTORY

ONE great cause of Henry's stability at home was his financial credit. In the first year of his reign he had asked the city for a loan of 6000 marks—that is to say, £4000—but the city only agreed to give him half the sum, which the king accepted graciously without showing any disappointment. It was punctually repaid, and in July 1488 the city advanced a further sum of £2000, or, according to another authority, £4000, which was duly repaid likewise. Henry could not but have seen that considerable caution was necessary in the matter of borrowing until the confidence rudely shaken by revolution and civil war had returned. But punctual repayment soon restored confidence, which no doubt was all the more confirmed as it became known that he was gradually accumulating treasure. Much of the money he laid by he appears to have invested in the purchase of jewels, which while they were in use added brilliance to his Court and at other times could be employed as security for further loans. Thus, during the first half of his reign, although certainly he was growing continually richer even then, his privy purse expenses show him to have been a very frequent borrower, as frequently repaying the sums advanced to him.

But when the war with France appeared imminent he found it necessary to have further aid of his subjects than by way of loan, and notwithstanding the Act of Richard III., he resolved to have it by way of benevolence.   Nor did he even ask authority to do so from Parliament, as Lord Bacon informs us that he did—at all events, not from what we should call a Parliament now. The body to which he applied was really a Great Council only.   Great Councils, often loosely called Parliaments, had often been summoned at important crises in public affairs, and as they consisted of lords and leading men and representatives of important towns, the weight of their decisions was hardly inferior to that of Parliament itself.   So that when about June 1491 a Great Council sanctioned the revival of benevolences with a view to the coming war, the decision, though it could hardly have been popular, appears to have been acquiesced in by the nation without a murmur.

The legal objection probably did not stand very much in the way.   The war was clearly in accordance with the wishes of the nation, and the method of raising funds was not an unreasonable one in itself, provided there was no undue pressure amounting to extortion. Manifestly, however, a direct application from the head of the State to private individuals and wealthy corporations for money was a practice very liable to abuse, and all the more so when it had received a kind of sanction almost equivalent to that of statute law.   No one thought of disputing the authority of the commission, and the instructions given to the commissioners were so cunningly worded that the pressure brought upon individuals was severely felt. Cardinal Morton had the credit of drawing up these instructions; and one article suggested an argument familiarly known as "Morton's fork." In it the commissioners were directed, according to Lord Bacon, "that if they met any that were sparing they should tell them that they must needs have, because they laid up; and if they were spenders they must needs have, because it was seen in their port and manner of living; so neither kind came amiss." Arguments like this were a little cruel; and they were felt all the more so when it appeared by the sequel that the king, to use the language of Lord Bacon again, had only "trafficked with that war," making thereby a double profit, "upon his subjects for the war, and upon his enemies for the peace." His subjects, however, had not all paid in advance; and as the demand was, strictly speaking, illegal, those who had not done so before naturally expected to keep their money to themselves when the peace with France was concluded. But they were not allowed to escape so easily; for three years later Henry obtained an Act giving retrospective validity to the exaction, and compelling every one who was in arrear to pay up the full amount that he had promised.

This may be regarded as the beginning of those extortions which formed such a painful feature of Henry's reign, for it was in the same year as this Act of Parliament that Alderman Sir William Capel first fell a victim to the pettifogging ingenuity of Sir Richard Empson, and was condemned in the sum of £2700 under certain obsolete penal laws, though he was allowed to compound with the king for £1600. This and the

long series of later persecutions with which the names
of Empson and Dudley are associated, appear to have
been due to a double policy, having two aims, each
of great importance to a king in Henry's position —
first to enforce a higher respect for law, and secondly
to fill his treasury in a way that could not be complained of. It was a considerable object with the king
to secure for himself an ample reserve of treasure
without burdening his subjects at large with too severe
taxation. The desire of Englishmen, and even of statesmen and judges like Sir John Fortescue, for a whole
generation and more, had been to see their king "live of
his own," so as to make parliamentary grants unnecessary;
and Henry realised more clearly than any previous
sovereign that money was a source of power. He kept
his own accounts very carefully, and many of his account-
books remain to this day with annotations in his own
hand as to particular items of income and expenditure.

But to make the law feared was a still greater object
than to fill his treasury, and while many and even serious
offences could be compounded for, it was necessary that
in prominent cases severity should be used. For the dis-
closures made by Sir Robert Clifford as to the intrigues
at home in favour of Perkin Warbeck it was the general
opinion that Henry was very well prepared beforehand,
and in particular that he had long suspected the guilt
of Sir William Stanley. Of the extent of that guilt
it is difficult for the modern reader to form any clear
estimate, because there is no record of the precise acts
or sayings of which he was found guilty. Every one
knows that the law of treason was in those days severely
interpreted; and the tradition reported by Lord Bacon

may be true that the case against him rested merely on his having said to Sir Robert Clifford that if he were sure the young man (Warbeck) was King Edward's son, he would never bear arms against him. But a contemporary writer says expressly that Stanley had promised to help Perkin with money ; and this is really more likely in itself, as it is very improbable that Henry would have needlessly put to death the man who had rescued him from danger on the field of battle, and whom he had in consequence made his chamberlain.

The people were simply appalled by his execution, especially those who had in any way committed themselves to the cause of the pretender or of the House of York. For, apart from the consideration of past services and of the high honour in which he seemed to be held, there was a sort of affinity between Stanley and the king, inasmuch as his brother, the Earl of Derby, had married the king's mother, the Countess of Richmond ; so that the blow struck home, and could not but be felt grievously even by those most nearly related to the Crown. Henry, indeed, must have felt that he was to some extent chastising himself. His object, however, was to show that no such ties could be pleaded in mitigation of condign punishment in a matter which concerned not only his own safety but the peace of the kingdom as well. In fact the offence was greatly aggravated by these very circumstances, and whatever pain it might give, he was determined that the sentence should be carried out. It was done, and no doubt the result was salutary in the long run, but it led, as a first effect, to the diffusion of a multitude of libels, containing invectives against the king and his Council, for the dispersion of

which five men were apprehended and after examination
put to death.

It was perhaps the more important, after Sir William
Stanley's case, that the king should show his desire to
rule with clemency ; and in the Parliament which met
in October he caused a law to be passed, so little in
keeping with the spirit of those times that even Lord
Bacon, writing more than a century later, calls it "of a
strange nature, rather just than legal, and more magnanimous than provident." It was to protect from impeach-
ment, and even from attainder by Act of Parliament in
future, all who fought for a _de facto_ king, whatever
might be thought of his title afterwards. For it seemed
unjust that a subject should be punished for his allegiance even to a usurper like Richard III., who had a
right to command his services, and might have punished
him if he withheld them. Otherwise it was the duty of
every subject to investigate the king's title,—a doctrine
which it would have been dangerous even to insinuate
in those days. The enactment, therefore, was indisput-
ably just, the objection that it was not "legal" being
merely founded on the fact that one Parliament can
never tie the hands of succeeding Parliaments as to
attainders or any other questions. But when Bacon
adds that it was "more magnanimous than politic," we
may perhaps be permitted to doubt whether a mind like
his, great as it was in many things, fully appreciated
magnanimity even as a matter of policy. No doubt, as
he observes, it might weaken the hold the king had over
his own party by protecting their lives and fortunes
whether they fought for him strenuously or not; but, as
he likewise remarks, "it could not but greatly draw

unto him the love and hearts of the people, because he seemed more careful for them than for himself." Moreover, "it did the better take away occasion for the people to busy themselves to pry into the king's title, for, howsoever it fell, their safety was already provided for." Thus Bacon himself seems to answer his own criticism. The terror expressed by the Croyland monk, even at the comparatively few attainders at the beginning of Henry's reign, had hardly counterbalanced the sense of injustice that they aroused, and the new law, though it did not exclude all risk, was doubtless a very effective means of counteracting Yorkist intrigues.

It was in this Parliament that the Act was passed for compelling payment of arrears of the benevolence, which was artfully put as an act of justice towards those who had paid before, and was pretended to be passed at their request. But with it some wholesome enactments were made for the better administration of justice, especially to allow suing *in formâ pauperis*, which was a new remedy against oppression, and to punish juries returning false verdicts by a writ of attaint. Wholesome legislation, in fact, grew naturally with the sense of the king's security upon the throne, and it was clearly appreciated by his subjects that his interests were their own. It was only in this growing state of tranquillity that just laws could be passed, old iniquities redressed, and the precedents of legal severity put aside. The king was growing strong both at home and abroad. Perkin, who was now in Scotland, had been disowned by the archduke, and commerce was re-established with Flanders by the *Intercursus Magnus*. No English rebels could be harboured any more in the Netherlands, even in the lands of the Duchess Margaret; and with the exception of Charles VIII. and Maximilian (whose interests were opposed to each other and were safe to keep each other in check), there was not a prince on the Continent who did not assiduously cultivate friendly relations with England.

Scotland alone was a source of present trouble, and soon after the invasion of the Northern Marches by James and Perkin Warbeck, Henry called a Great Council at Westminster, to which all the principal towns in England sent representatives, and which, after sitting nearly a fortnight, agreed that the king should have a grant of £120,000 for defence against the Scots, and loans to the extent of £40,000 besides. The grant, it would seem, was only a recommendation to Parliament, which met within three months after, on the 16th of January 1497, and passed it in the form of a subsidy. But the king's agents at once set about soliciting the loan, first from the city of London and afterwards from other quarters throughout England; and notwithstanding that full payment of the benevolence had been recently extorted from everybody then in arrears, a sum of money seems to have been procured about £18,000 in excess of that which he had been authorised to borrow. Bacon's remark that Henry's wars "were always to him as a mine of treasure" is fully borne out by the accounts of this loan.

But a loan first and a subsidy afterwards, both following rather close upon the compulsory payment of the arrears of a benevolence, created naturally not a little irritation. The hardy men of Cornwall, in particular, began to murmur at these repeated exactions, and said it was intolerable to be thus ground down merely on account of "a little stir of the Scots, soon blown over." A lawyer named Thomas Flammock added to the excitement by telling them that a subsidy for such a purpose was unprecedented, if not illegal; that the legitimate way of obtaining service in war was by the old feudal custom of escuage; and that the case was such as to justify a strong remonstrance to the king, which might be made by a large body of Cornishmen going up to London, armed merely in self-defence. As usual in dangerous movements of this kind, the malcontents were to disown any thought of disloyalty; they would merely pray for the removal of those councillors (Morton and Bray were intended) who had given the king mischievous advice. A blacksmith or farrier of Bodmin named Michael Joseph was no less busy than Flammock in fanning the flames, and the two put themselves at the head of the expedition that was to march to London. A rude multitude, armed chiefly with bows and arrows, bills, and other simple weapons, passed onwards through Devonshire peacefully enough till they came to Taunton, in Somersetshire, where they killed a commissioner for the subsidy. At Wells they were joined by a nobleman, Lord Audley, who then became their leader and conducted them to Salisbury and Winchester. Finding no resistance as they advanced, they expressed a desire to be led into Kent, where the people, Flammock said, were the freest in all England. But the men of Kent, though they had given trouble enough to previous kings under a Wat Tyler or Jack Cade, had been only moved to sedition by injustice and disorderly government. They had no sympathy with rebellion against legally authorised taxation, and were encouraged to persevere in their loyalty by the king's approbation. So the insurgents, though they reached the borders of the county, found even less sympathy there than they had done elsewhere along their line of march.

The rising took the king by surprise and put him in some perplexity, seeing that he was at that very time sending an army northward against the Scots, under Lord Daubeney. These troops he recalled, and sent the Earl of Surrey into the north merely to defend the country in case the Scots should stir, while he himself left Sheen and proceeded westward as far as Woodstock. But he forbore to attack the rebels, deeming it more prudent that they should be allowed to march on a long way from their own country, and thus wear themselves out before joining battle. One little encounter, however, they had with Lord Daubeney's troops near Guildford. At last they encamped upon Blackheath, in full view of London. Henry meanwhile had gradually returned from Woodstock, and joined Lord Daubeney in St. George's Fields. The city, which was at first somewhat alarmed, was now reassured; for besides the king's own forces and those of Lord Daubeney, there were other detachments near at hand, commanded by the Earls of Oxford, Essex, and Suffolk. On the morning of Saturday, the 17th of June, these were directed to encircle the rebels where they lay, while Daubeney advanced upon them direct from the side towards London. The rebels, already disheartened by not meeting with so much sympathy as they expected from Kent, were soon put to flight, although Daubeney at the beginning of the action was for a while surrounded and in considerable danger.

Of their company, amounting, as it was said, to 15,000, no less than 2000 were slain. The rest were taken alive; among whom were the three leaders—Lord Audley, the blacksmith, and Flammock.

Henry used his victory with extreme moderation. Lord Audley was executed on Tower Hill after being led through the city in a torn paper coat painted with his own arms reversed. Flammock and the blacksmith were hanged, drawn, and quartered at Tyburn. But, with the exception of the three leaders, all the rest were pardoned—a clemency in marked contrast to the severe punishment of Perkin's followers captured after their landing at Deal, who had been executed to the number of one hundred and fifty. But there was all the difference in the world between men who, being severely taxed and deluded by popular oratory, had yet passed through the land in orderly and quiet fashion till it came to a pitched battle, and a mercenary crew of ruffians engaged to support an adventurer. Yet it is questionable whether Henry's lenity on this occasion was not a little in excess of what was politic, for it seems rather to have emboldened the Cornishmen to further acts of disloyalty. The king, they said, could not afford to be severe, for if he hanged all who objected to taxation as much as they did, he would have very few subjects left. They had begun to sympathise with Perkin Warbeck, who in his proclamation had glanced at the king's extortions and promised to put an end to them. They accordingly sent messages over to Ireland, where Perkin now was, intimating that if he would only land in Cornwall he would be sure to find plenty of followers.

The message wonderfully revived the drooping spirits
of Perkin and his Council, of whom the three leading
members were Heron, a mercer who had fled for debt;
Skelton, a tailor; and Astley, a scrivener. The unprofitable
campaign in Ireland was at once abandoned for a descent
on Cornwall, whither Perkin and his little company
found their way in four small barks, which seem to have
narrowly escaped capture on the voyage. They landed
at Whitesand Bay in September, and went on to Bodmin,
where about 3000 of the Cornish people actually joined
them. A march on Exeter was naturally the next move
in the game, and cajolery was employed to induce
the city to be the first to open its gates to one who
claimed their allegiance as their lawful sovereign. The
citizens, however, paid little regard to this appeal, and
prepared to make good their defence till succour came
from the king. The rebels were without artillery, and
the only thing they could do was to set fire to one of
the city gates. But before the fire had burned down to
clear a passage for the besiegers the citizens piled up a
great barrier of faggots and other fuel, which continued
to burn while they made ramparts and trenches within.
So the besiegers gained no advantage by their attempt
upon the gate, and their efforts to scale the walls were
equally unsuccessful.

Perkin must have known very well by this time that
his cause was hopeless, and that his long career was
coming to a close. Often as he had gained support
abroad, or in Scotland or Ireland, he had but once been
on English ground before, and his pretended subjects
would have nothing to do with him. Now he had
landed in England again, and although he received en-

couragement from those who were disaffected already, he
doubtless saw that in the end the result would be much
the same—only that he was never again to escape and
seek sympathy with foreign princes. The king rejoiced
at the news of his advance on Exeter, feeling that his
retreat was now practically cut off. He sent Lord Daubeney, Lord Willoughby de Broke, and others at once
to succour the town; but before their arrival in the
west the Earl of Devonshire and his son, with the local
gentry, made haste to do the work uncommissioned,
while the Duke of Buckingham and many others ten-
dered their services to the king with such forces as they
too had got ready. Fearing to be surrounded at Exeter,
Perkin led his men on to Taunton, in Somersetshire,
making as if he were ready to fight his way to London.
But during the night he escaped with a small company
of horsemen to Beaulieu Abbey, in Hampshire, where he
and his attendants took the benefit of sanctuary. The
sanctuary was soon surrounded by a body of horse, sent
by the king in the hope of intercepting them before they
reached it, and Perkin remained a prisoner till further
orders.

His followers, deserted by their leader, naturally submitted to the king's mercy without striking a blow, and
Henry marched on to Exeter, where he was joyfully
received, and presented his own sword to the mayor, to
be carried before him thenceforth in processions. A few
of the Cornish ringleaders were executed for the trouble
they had given to the city, and counsel was taken what
to do with Perkin himself. There was some argument
for taking him out of sanctuary by force and putting
him to death, an act which the Pope could easily have

M

been got to ratify by an indulgence. But this would have made the adventurer of too great importance, and the king preferred to spare his life and obtain from him a full confession of his imposture. He was sent up to London and paraded through the streets on horseback amid much hooting and derision of the citizens; and he made a full confession, which the king caused to be printed and sent about the country, showing who he was and what his life had been; giving also the precise names of his father, mother, and various other relations at Tournay. His wife, Katharine Gordon, whom he had left behind him at St. Michael's Mount, was sent for by the king when he was at Exeter, and received from him the consideration due to her rank, her beauty, and her misfortunes. He sent her to keep company with his queen, and gave her an allowance to maintain herself with, which she continued to enjoy long after the king's death.

This time Henry did not give a free pardon to the rebels generally, but he adopted a mode of punishment both merciful and characteristic. He appointed Lord Darcy and others as commissioners to impose fines—great or little, according to the value of their property—on those who had given any countenance either to Michael Joseph or to Perkin, thus showing that he was not daunted, as they had expected him to be, by the previous rising against taxation. The commissioners went through the whole of the western counties, hundred by hundred. No one who had been in any way implicated in the rebellion was passed over, many abbots and heads of religious houses, among others, being obliged to compound for their pardon. The payments, however, were only to be made by instalments

during years to come, so that men felt that they were
personally answerable for their good behaviour long after
the rising was put down. The proceeds of the fines
were entered upon special rolls, of which at least two
remain to us, not referring to the counties most seriously
in fault, but only to Somerset, Dorset, Wiltshire, and
Hampshire. Their added totals amount to over £13,000,
and from two memoranda in the king's own hand it
appears that the first levy of the money was to be at
Easter 1501, three and a half years after the rebellion,
and that the last payment made by one of the collectors,
Sherbourne, Dean of St. Paul's, who had by that time
become Bishop of St. David's, into the royal treasury
was a sum of £80 still remaining due on the 24th of
March 1506.

CHAPTER XI

PROSPERITY AND ALLIANCES

THE capture and confession of Perkin Warbeck put an end to the chief source of trouble that Henry had yet encountered, and covered with confusion the intrigues of his enemies abroad. And just about the same time, after an unpleasant revival of hostilities with Scotland, a seven years' truce was at length made with some faint hope of a lasting settlement.

It was not effected, we are told, without a great deal of discussion, and this we can readily believe. The inveterate hostility between the two countries was not easily eradicated; and the arts by which Henry had sought to keep James in check were not altogether laudable. He had an understanding with the Earl of Angus, who pledged himself under certain circumstances to take the part of England against his own sovereign. He had a spy at the Scotch Court in the person of Lord Bothwell, a favourite minister of James III., who had never forgiven the reigning king his complicity in the rebellion against his father. Bothwell had induced James IV.'s own brother, the Duke of Ross, the Earl of Buchan, and the Bishop of Moray to promise Henry their assistance in frustrating any attempt to invade England. He had

also arranged a plot for the kidnapping of Warbeck in
his tent while he was in Scotland and sending him up to
Henry   Such underhand conspiracies were evidently
considered justifiable as a means of counteracting the
designs of an enemy like the Scots, who were habitually
reproached by their southern neighbours with bad faith
in treaties.   And it must be owned that the reproach
was not altogether unmerited; for it was difficult to deal
with a nation whose cohesion was so loose among themselves that they were not wholly subject to authority,
and among whom there was at all times a strong party
against England, to which even pacific kings, if they had
such, could not but occasionally give way.

James IV. was a king possessed of many noble qualities, as well as of many accomplishments hardly to be
looked for in one so far removed from continental civili-
sation.   He was not only a good Latin scholar, and
could talk Gaelic with the Highlanders as well as Low-
land Scotch, but he had the command of all the leading
European languages.   A student of nature and a lover
of experiment, his acquaintance with medicine and sur-
gery seems to have been more than respectable for those
days.   His strict observance of religious ordinances was
no doubt quickened by the remorse he felt for the part
he had taken against his father.   His temperance both
in eating and drinking was almost unexampled.   His
sincerity, truthfulness, and love of justice made him an
admirable ruler; while his humanity, courage, and
bravery endeared him to his subjects.   But he was a
lover of war, even for its own sake.   He personally
enjoyed its dangers; and he was not the man to think
lightly of any provocation he received that might kindle

anew those flames whose violence both Henry and Ferdinand were so anxious to assuage.

Henry's astute councillor, Richard Fox, Bishop of
Durham, whose diocese was much exposed to the incur-
sions of the Scots, had done his best to compose the differences between the two kingdoms. He had negotiated
on the Borders with Angus and Lord Hume, who, though
committed to a certain extent to Henry's interests, could
not offer on their sovereign's behalf terms entirely to his
satisfaction; for James would not agree to surrender
Warbeck, a point on which Henry absolutely insisted, so
long as the adventurer remained in Scotland. Nor was
it with any avowed aim of facilitating a peace that he
finally thought it expedient to send him away; for
immediately afterwards he again invaded England in
person and laid siege to Norham. Fox, however, who
had beforehand strongly garrisoned the castle and prepared it to stand a siege, gave notice at once to the Earl
of Surrey, the king's Lieutenant of the North, then in
Yorkshire, to come to the rescue; who thereupon summoned all the powerful noblemen of the northern counties
—such as the Earl of Westmoreland, Lords Dacre,
Nevill, Clifford, Lumley, Darcy, and many others, with
the principal gentry—to join his standard, and was soon
at the head of a force of nearly 20,000 men, while a fleet
under Lord Willoughby de Broke was sent northwards
to assist the expedition by sea.

On hearing of the approach of this great army James
felt it necessary to abandon the siege of Norham and
retire within his own realm. Surrey entered Scotland,
threw down a number of fortresses, and summoned the
Captain of Ayton Castle, one of the strongest places

between Berwick and Edinburgh, to yield it up. The captain refused, hoping for succours, and ere long King James and his army drew nigh. But James, seeing, no doubt, that the force at his command was quite inadequate to cope with the English forces, offered to settle the questions in controversy by a single combat between him and Surrey, in which, if he were victorious, the earl was to deliver to him as his ransom the town of Berwick, with the fish-garths belonging to it. The earl said he was highly honoured by such a challenge from so noble a king, and would be delighted to accept it, but the town of Berwick was not his own; it belonged to the king his master. The earl accordingly prepared to meet the onset of the Scots, but James withdrew his army in the night season. Surrey, on the other hand, finding he could not maintain so large an army in that barren, inhospitable country, the weather, too, being extremely foul and tempestuous, withdrew for a time to Berwick. Meanwhile peace negotiations were resumed. The Scots, under the influence of Don Pedro de Ayala, were at length brought to reason; and the seven years' truce was concluded at Ayton on the 30th of September 1497.

Ayala feared greatly that, notwithstanding the pacific disposition of the English king and of Fox, Bishop of Durham, the truce would not last so long. The Borderers were not easy to control, and James's high spirit would rather seek than avoid an opportunity of renewing hostilities. And in fact, just about a twelvemonth later, the work of the peacemakers was very nearly undone by an incident which occurred on the banks of the Tweed at Norham. It was observed that some Scotch gentlemen crossed the river on two successive days,

apparently to view the castle. They were fully armed,
and being asked their object, replied with haughty
words not likely to allay suspicions. Blows were
presently exchanged, and the Scotchmen, being on
foreign ground, naturally had the worst of it. Several
of them were wounded and some killed; the rest took
flight. Redress was demanded of the Wardens of the
Marches, but their procedure did not satisfy King James,
who, swearing "by sweet St. Ninian" that there was no
reliance to be placed on Englishmen for the observance
of the peace, sent up Marchmont Herald to Henry with
an angry message. Nor was he greatly softened on
receiving an answer as conciliatory as could reasonably
have been expected; for Henry was really vexed at the
occurrence, and promised full inquiry and punishment
of the offenders if any of his subjects were found to be
in fault. But the work of pacification lay with Bishop
Fox, who, heartily desiring the preservation of peace,
sent many letters to the Scotch king expressive of the
utmost possible regret, and assuring him that no
countenance would be given by his sovereign to any acts
tending to the renewal of hostilities.

Fox doubtless had made a favourable impression upon
James already, and he not only succeeded in appeasing
his anger, but was requested to come and confer with
him in his own kingdom as to the best means of promot-
ing more amicable relations between the two countries.
On receiving Henry's authority for this purpose the
bishop repaired to Melrose, where James gave him an
interview, and after the Norham incident had been fully
apologised for in presence of the Scotch Council, spoke
with him apart on the possibility of inducing Henry, in

whose counsels he knew that the bishop had great influence, to give him his eldest daughter Margaret in
marriage. Fox promised to advànce the project to the
utmost of his power, and on repairing to Henry urged
the conclusion of a regular peace, to be followed by a
treaty for the marriage. All which took effect in due
time, the treaty being made on the 12th of July next
year (1499), and the bishop himself receiving a commission to negotiate the marriage on the 11th of September
following.

Meanwhile the death of Charles VIII. of France had
created a new state of things in Europe. Its immediate
effect seemed likely to be to weaken France by separating once more the duchy of Britanny from the French
Crown. For Charles's only son had died before him, and
his widowed queen was still Duchess of Britanny in her
own right. And to Britanny she actually returned, to
resume her sovereignty there, issuing edicts and assem-
bling the Estates of the duchy as in the days of old.
The new king, however, Louis XII., had known very
well, even in past times, what the independence of
Britanny meant to the French monarchy; for he was
that Louis, Duke of Orleans, who had taken refuge in
the duchy during Charles VIII.'s minority, and stirred
up trouble from thence for the regent, Madame de
Beaujeu. It was he too who in later years, when Charles
invaded Italy, had excited the jealousy of Ludovico
Sforza by putting forth an ancestral claim to the duchy
of Milan, and was accordingly shut up for a time in
Novara. What was he going to do now as King of
France? In spite of past mishaps, endeavour to make
Milan a fief of the French Crown? And if foreign

princes took alarm once more, how was he going to
secure himself on the side of Britanny, where England
and Spain would again come to the rescue if the duchess
called for aid ?   His policy in these matters remained for
a while a secret, but ere long it was very distinctly
unfolded.

His first aim was to secure the friendship of England,
not merely for fear of interference in Britanny (where he
had reasons not known to the world as yet for believing
himself tolerably safe), but with a view to promote
division among the confederates in the Holy League.
He accordingly sent, immediately after his accession,
first a king-at-arms and then a regular embassy to
Henry ; but Henry declined to treat with him apart
from Spain, and sent spies over both to France and to
Britanny to see what factions were likely to arise, and
whether it would be an advantageous time to attack.
Louis, however, made it his next object to win the
favour of Pope Alexander VI., so as not only to detach
his Holiness from the league, but also to procure for
himself a divorce from his queen, Jeanne, daughter of
Louis XI., in order that he might marry Anne of
Britanny, and secure himself on that side also.   Political
reasons had begun to be recognised at the Papal Court
as sufficient in certain cases for separating man and wife
or for permitting marriages within prohibited degrees ;
and the policy of maintaining the union between France
and Britanny was held to be a sufficient justification in
this case.   Not that the bull was issued from this consideration alone.   Louis quite expected that *some* scruples
would be raised as to such an extreme exercise of pon-
tifical power, but he knew also how to allay them.   He

created Cæsar Borgia, the Pope's too notorious son, Duke of Valentinois, and desired the Pope to send him into France, where he might take possession of his duchy, and to send the bull along with him. There was no opposition, and in the course of a few months the thing was done. Louis had got rid of his old wife and married Anne of Britanny. He had, moreover, broken up the league. Henry VII. saw that none of the Italian powers was to be depended on. Ludovico Sforza had become of small account. The Venetians were preparing to follow the Pope's example, and very soon did so. Louis had also won over the Archduke Philip as an ally, while his father, Maximilian, remained hostile, fearing what would evidently soon take place—a second French descent upon Italy, which the Italian powers generally, with the single exception of Sforza, seemed very well disposed to welcome. Not one of the confederates had much regard for the other, except England and Spain; and even these two each agreed to make peace with France on terms approved by the other—rather better terms in Henry's case than he had exacted from Charles VIII.

So the way was cleared for Louis to invade Italy and make good his claim to Milan, whose duke, Ludovico Sforza, he ultimately shut up in a French prison; to invade it again and divide with Ferdinand the kingdom of Naples, driving out the last successor of the Arragonese line of sovereigns, who had held the throne for more than forty years; to be then overreached by Ferdinand, and compelled ultimately to yield up Naples to him entirely. But these further issues concerned England comparatively little, their importance in after years

being mainly in connection with events which have yet
to be referred to.

Meanwhile, but for one or two uncomfortable inci-
dents, Henry might be said to have reached the climax
of his prosperity. He was at peace with all his neighbours, and had a good understanding especially with
France, Spain, and the Archduke Philip. Warbeck was
for ever discredited by his own confession, and seems to
have been detained in some kind of lax custody about
the Court as one whom there was no occasion to punish
severely. Even Henry's Juno, the old Duchess of
Burgundy, was compelled to ask his pardon for the
support she had given to impostors. Negotiations for
the projected marriage of Prince Arthur with Katharine
of Arragon were proceeding rapidly with the utmost
goodwill on both sides ; and other negotiations, as we
have seen, were going on for a settled peace with
Scotland ; when first a somewhat disagreeable impression
was produced by an effort of Perkin to escape. He
took to his heels "without any reason," as the Spanish
ambassador remarked, and made for the sea-coast. The
thing caused a momentary flutter ; but pursuit was
made, and diligent search wherever he was likely to
have gone, and he soon found it advisable to give up his
attempt and take sanctuary at the Priory of Sheen.
The prior begged his life of the king, who agreed to
spare him when delivered, and put him in the stocks,
where he was exhibited first at Westminster and then
in Cheapside ; after which he was committed to the
Tower for greater security in future.

Perhaps the king really did mean at that time to
spare his life, for he was too contemptible an object in

himself to be worth putting to death. But very shortly
after the madness of faction was exhibited in the setting
up of a new pretender, Ralph Wilford, who was educated
by an Augustinian friar, to personate the imprisoned
Earl of Warwick. Rash and hopeless as the attempt
was, it touched the king in the sorest point of his apprehensions, for it showed that the wrong he had done to
the earl in keeping him in prison had not mitigated the
danger of Yorkist conspiracies in his favour. Wilford
was hanged in February 1499; but in March it was
observed that Henry had come to look twenty years
older in the course of a single fortnight. A report, too,
not altogether unworthy of credit, said that he had con-
sulted a priest, who was credited with the gift of
prophecy, how long he had to live, and received answer
that his life would be in danger for a whole year. He
grew particularly devout. The time of year was Lent,
and he listened to a sermon every day besides other
observances. But one dark thought was certainly
haunting his mind, destined to bear unpleasant fruit in
the course of a very few months.

Warbeck's place of confinement in the Tower was not
far removed from that of the Earl of Warwick, and
it could hardly have been quite an accident that the
two found themselves able to communicate with each
other. Warbeck, in fact, either drew his gaolers, or,
as is more likely, was drawn by some of them, into a
plot for his own and the Earl of Warwick's liberation.
The poor earl, who was but four-and-twenty years old,
and had been from early boyhood continually in prison,
knew nothing of the world, and yielded an easy assent
to a project framed in his own interest. Of course the

matter was soon disclosed, and of course also it was then quite clear that it involved much more than an attempt to break from prison. Gathering together all the fragments of private conversation sworn to by the informers, it would have been strange if the Crown lawyers had not been able to twist out of them a design to levy war against the king. The earl was formally charged with a conspiracy to seize the Tower and make himself king, and Warbeck was indicted as his accomplice. That the former was absolutely innocent of any such design, even if the plan was not in itself preposterous, was admitted frankly in the Act by which his attainder was reversed in the succeeding reign. But it was clear his life had to be sacrificed to a supposed necessity of State, and the thing was done with all judicial formalities. He was duly tried before his peers, the Earl of Oxford acting as High Constable of England, and being found guilty, was beheaded a week after on Tower Hill; while Perkin and three of his accomplices expiated their offences at Tyburn.

We are told by Bacon that Henry, to shield himself to some extent from unpleasant comments on the subject of Warwick's death, caused letters from Spain to be shown, in which Ferdinand wrote plainly "that he saw no assurance of his succession as long as the Earl of Warwick lived, and that he was loth to send his daughter to troubles and dangers." This is probably an over-statement, for the diplomatic correspondence between Spain and England is now pretty fully known to us, and there is no trace in it of any such explicit declaration. But we do find by that correspondence that very great importance was attached by the Spanish ambassador, if not

by his master, to the Earl of Warwick's execution, and
to the fact that there remained in the kingdom "not a
doubtful drop of royal blood," or any possible rival by
inheritance to the claims of the king and queen ; so that
Prince Arthur's right to the succession would be undisputed.   The kingdom, De Puebla assured Ferdinand,
was now really more secure than it had been for five
hundred years.

The Spanish sovereigns were of the same opinion.
They were now more convinced than ever of the value
of Henry as an ally, and they readily ratified two new
treaties which had been drawn up in London, the one
for a political alliance and the other for the marriage.
Henry on his side was eager that Katharine should be
sent to England that very year (1500) ; but his councillors were more particular about the terms of the new
alliance than those of Ferdinand and Isabella, and De
Puebla declared that after long negotiations he had
almost despaired of satisfying them.   Henry had in the
meantime gone over to Calais, partly perhaps, as men
supposed, to avoid the plague then raging in London.
But another object was to lure the Archduke Philip to
an interview, which accordingly took place between them
at St. Peter's church, just outside Calais ; for Philip declined to enter a walled town, as he had refused to do
so already at the French king's invitation, and although
he professed greater confidence in Henry, he would not
establish a bad precedent.   And this interview seems to
have led, for the time at least, to important results in
the way of cementing old alliances and making them
more cordial, for there had recently been commercial
disputes between the two countries.   To crown all, after

various conferences, an agreement was come to for a
marriage between Henry, Duke of York, the king's
second son, and a daughter of the archduke ; and another
between the archduke's son and heir Charles (afterwards
the Emperor Charles V.), at that time not four months
old, and Henry's second daughter Mary.   Neither of
these matches ultimately took effect, but the second was
persistently kept in view for many years, and was not
dropped for some time after Henry VII.'s death.

But when the news of Henry's crossing to Calais—or
perhaps of his intention to go thither—reached Ferdinand and Isabella, it put them for a time in a considerable state of alarm.   What was the meaning of it ? Was
the marriage between Arthur and Katharine, to which
Henry had so fully pledged himself, and which, in fact,
had been already celebrated more than once by proxy,
going to be set aside in favour of some better offer from
Maximilian, King of the Romans ?   Ferdinand could
not help judging others by his own standard in such
matters, and despatched a special ambassador in hot
haste through France to Henry, the real object of whose
mission was only to spy out truths that he could not
trust even De Puebla to communicate.   And in truth as
the envoy neared Calais, from which Henry before his
arrival had already taken ship again for England, he
heard pretty definite rumours that a marriage had been
positively concluded between the Prince of Wales and
Maximilian's daughter Margaret, now the widow of
Ferdinand and Isabella's son Juan, who had just returned from Spain to Flanders.   There was, however,
no real ground for the rumour ; and though Henry, at
the urgent request of the Spanish sovereigns, agreed to

allow Katharine's voyage to England to be delayed till
next year, there was no further obstacle to the consum-
mation of the marriage.

Meanwhile there came to England from Pope Alexander VI. a nuncio, named Gaspar Pons, to distribute to
those who were not able to visit Rome in that year of
jubilee (1500) the indulgences they might have gained
by doing so, on their making a sufficient contribution to
the papal treasury.   Pons also brought a brief from the
Pope to urge him to enter on a crusade in person against
the Turks, whose progress in Europe was creating considerable alarm; insomuch that there were fears that
they might land in Italy and even drive the Pope from
Rome.   To this object it was intimated that the sum
collected for the indulgence would be applied.   Henry,
though he allowed the money to be collected, replied to
this appeal for a crusade with a letter of polite excuse, in
which, besides pleading the long distance and the time
and expense that would be involved in his case in fitting
out and sending an expedition, he rather insinuated that
even if the Turk did come to Italy it would not greatly
disturb his repose in England.   But in truth he was not
so indifferent to the project if he could only see it carried
out in good faith.   It was thought by many that he
shared the proceeds of the collection made for the Pope
in his kingdom.   This was what all other princes did by
arrangement with the Holy See; but Henry did not.
He ultimately handed over £4000 to the papal nuncio,
though he had some correspondence before doing so with
Ferdinand of Spain as to the possibility of using the money
really for its ostensible purpose, and keeping it out of
the Pope's clutches, who would certainly use it otherwise.

That Henry was most in earnest of all princes about
the defence of Christendom against the Turk seems to
have been recognised by the Knights of Rhodes, who
constituted him protector of their order. If there was
yet some reality anywhere in the old crusading sentiment it was in him, and towards the end of his reign,
instead of waiting to be exhorted by the Pope, he positively urged the project upon Julius II., when the latter,
seeing no prospect of a union among Christian princes,
took the matter more coolly.

To return to the Spanish marriage. Katharine at
length left the Court of her parents at Granada in May
1501 for Coruña, where she was to embark. Even the
land journey was slow, from the intense heat, and after
taking ship she was obliged by adverse winds to return
to Spain. At last, however, the voyage was successfully
accomplished, and she landed at Plymouth on the 2d of
October. No pains or cost had been spared to give her
a magnificent reception, and on the 14th of November
she was married to Prince Arthur at St. Paul's amid
universal rejoicings.

Prince Arthur was at the time little more than fifteen
years of age; Katharine a year older. The extreme
youth of the prince, and possibly some appearance of a
weakly constitution, rendered it advisable, in the opinion
of some at least of the Council, to delay their cohabita·
tion; and though Henry wrote to Ferdinand and Isabella
as if for Katharine's sake he had overruled this advice,
there is considerable ground for believing that it was
really acted upon. The young couple, however, were
not kept very far apart, but were sent down together to
the borders of Wales, where the Princes of Wales were

accustomed to hold their Court to keep order in the marches. Here they seem to have spent barely three or, at the utmost, four months together, when their union was dissolved by a painful and unexpected blow. But this perhaps had better be related in the words of an unknown contemporary, whose brief narrative of the fact and the reception of the news at Court is invaluable, as showing us the more human aspects of a character often represented untruly as cold and unloving :—

" In the year of our Lord God 1502, the second day of April, in the castle of Ludlow, deceased Prince Arthur, first begotten son of our Sovereign Lord, King Henry the Seventh, and in the 17th year of his reign. Immediately after his death Sir Richard Poole, his chamberlain, with other of his Council, wrote and sent letters to the King and Council to Greenwich, where his Grace and the Queen's lay, and certified them of the Prince's departure. The which Council discreetly sent for the King's ghostly father, a friar Observant, to whom they showed this most sorrowful and heavy tidings, and desired him in his best manner to show it to the King. He in the morning of the Tuesday following, somewhat before the time accustomed, knocked at the King's chamber door ; and when the King understood it was his Confessor, he commanded to let him in. The Confessor then commanded all those there present to avoid, and after due salutation began to say, *Si bona de manu Dei suscipimus, mala autem quare non sustineamus ?*[1] and so showed his Grace that his dearest son was departed to God. When his Grace understood that sorrowful heavy tidings he sent for the Queen, saying that he and his queen would take the painful sorrows together. After that she was come, and saw the King her lord and that natural and painful sorrow, as I have heard say, she with full great, and constant comfortable words besought his Grace

---

[1] " If we receive good things at the hand of God, why may we not endure evil things ?"—Job ii. 10. The translation in our English Bible differs slightly in the form of expression.

that he would, first after God, remember the weal of his own noble person, the comfort of his realm and of her. She then said that my lady his mother had never no more children but him only, and that God by his grace had ever preserved him and brought him where that he was : over that, how that God had left him yet a fair prince, two fair princesses ; and that God is where he was, and we are both young enough ; and that the prudence and wisdom of his Grace sprung over all Christendom, so that it should please him to take this accordingly thereunto. Then the King thanked her of her good comfort. After that she was departed and come to her own chamber, natural and motherly remembrance of that great loss smote her so sorrowful to the heart, that those that were about her were fain to send for the King to comfort her. Then his Grace, of true, gentle, and faithful love, in good haste came and relieved her and showed her how wise counsel she had given him before ; and he for his part would thank God for his son, and would she should do in like wise."

No doubt, being a politician above all things, Henry, after these first emotions were over, must have thought seriously what was now to be done with Katharine, how she was henceforth to live, and whether she should be sent back to Spain. But it was her father who, as soon as the news reached him, was most deeply concerned, first about his daughter, and secondly, perhaps not less, about the marriage portion given along with her. The amount of this was 200,000 scudos, of which as yet he had only paid one-half ; for it had been arranged that only one-half was to be paid at first, the rest being payable afterwards in two instalments, and that Henry, to whom the whole was made over by an act of renunciation on Katharine's part, should receive the third instalment in plate and jewels, which the princess brought along with her, at a just valuation. Ferdinand, on carefully considering how matters now stood, came to the conclusion, first, that he was no longer called upon to pay any more ; and secondly, that Henry was bound to repay him even the first instalment of this dower, and at the same time to put Katharine in full possession of the lands and revenues set apart for her jointure, so that she should have no occasion to borrow for her necessary expenses. These demands, he considered, were fully borne out both by civil and by canon law ; but he evidently did not expect them to be complied with, and therefore empowered an ambassador, whom he sent to England on the business, to settle all disputes by the conclusion of a new marriage for Katharine with the king's second son, Henry, Duke of York, who afterwards (ten months after his brother's death) was created Prince of Wales in Arthur's place.

Henry, the father, did not see the justice of Ferdinand's demands. He was quite ready, even unasked, to put Katharine in possession of her jointure, but he demurred to the repayment of the first instalment of her dower, of which he considered the whole ought rightfully to come to him. The Spanish sovereigns had soon cause to feel that they had pitched their demands too high, and probably they regretted their mistake when they found immediately after that they wanted England's help again against France, which was making war upon them both in Naples and at Perpignan. Isabella in particular became most anxious that the second marriage should be concluded, and when Henry showed himself rather cool on this subject, instructed her ambassador to demand the return of Katharine to Spain, telling the king he had instructions to freight vessels for her voyage.

But while these matters were in suspense another

cloud passed over Henry's home, a heavier and darker
cloud than the death of Arthur. On the 11th of February
1503 he lost his queen, Elizabeth of York, a woman
much beloved by the people, who undoubtedly had
exercised much influence over him for good, although it
is true, in the words of Bacon, that towards her "he was
nothing uxorious." Henry, indeed, was too much a king
to be greatly under the control of women, and with
matters political she had certainly nothing to do. But
we notice a deterioration of Henry's character after
he became a widower; not that we hear of ordinary
scandals either before or after his bereavement, and it
may be that as regards these his life was pure. He was,
moreover, careful in the education of his children, and
the little glimpse of his family circle given us by Erasmus
is altogether pleasing. But we have many evidences that
towards the end of his days he yielded to coarser and
more sordid influences than he had done before. Nor
was the queen the only good friend and counsellor of
whom death had at this time deprived him; for Sir
Reginald Bray died about the same time, and Cardinal
Morton had passed away less than three years before.
And these were the men whose advice had prevailed
most in dissuading him from acts of tyranny.

A year before the queen's death, in January 1502,
the Earl of Bothwell, as proxy for James IV. of Scotland,
had solemnly espoused the Princess Margaret in his
master's name at Richmond. In June following she herself
was accompanied by her father from Richmond to Colly-
weston in Northamptonshire, on the way towards Scotland.   There he took leave of her on the 8th of July, and
from thence, moving northwards by slow stages accom-

panied by a splendid retinue, she was conducted to
Scotland by the Earl of Surrey, who was joined on the
way by the Earl of Northumberland and many of the
northern lords. On the 8th of August the marriage was
celebrated between the parties themselves at Edinburgh
—a union which, as the reader is well aware, ultimately
brought England and Scotland under the same Crown.

An interesting tradition in connection with the
negotiation of this marriage is recorded by Lord Bacon.
Some of Henry's Council are said to have put to him the
case which actually happened exactly a hundred years
afterwards, that owing to this marriage, on failure of the
issue of Henry's only surviving son, the future Henry
VIII., a King of Scotland might succeed to the English
throne. Would not this, it was suggested, be to the
prejudice of England? But Henry's answer was clear
that Scotland would in that case be an accession to
England, not England to Scotland, "for that the greater
would draw the less, and that it was a safer union for
England than that of France." It was a wise and
statesmanlike answer, and showed well, what was often
remarked of Henry, that he was quite free from ordinary
English prejudices.

CHAPTER XII

HENRY was still compelled to keep a watchful eye on the remaining branches of the House of York. True, all the male line of that family was extinct by the death of the Earl of Warwick. But the house of De la Pole, which had been disappointed by the overthrow of Richard III., not only of a prospect of the throne, but of high foreign alliances besides, still created some uneasiness. Its head, John de la Pole, Duke of Suffolk, who had married Edward IV.'s sister, had been dead many years. Not being of the blood-royal himself, he had never given offence, and had been treated by Henry with every mark of confidence, even after his son, the Earl of Lincoln, had taken part with Simnel. But the family estate was so reduced by Lincoln's attainder that when the second son, Edmund de la Pole, succeeded to the dukedom of Suffolk, he was glad to make a compromise with the king and content himself with the title of earl instead, on the restoration of some of the confiscated lands. Still he seems to have nursed his discontent in secret. He was a man of violent temper, and though he had studied at Oxford, was illiterate to a degree far beyond the ordinary standard of the nobility of those

days.   He was, however, expert in tournaments, and had
various showy qualities, for which he was admitted to
the order of the Garter.   He had, moreover, done good
service at Blackheath, and the king showed so much
regard for him as even to visit him once at his own
house at Ewelme.

But in 1498 he killed a man in a fury, and being
indicted for the homicide, he received the king's pardon.
He seems, however, to have felt it an indignity that he
was drawn into the king's Court at all.   After brooding
over the matter for some time, he escaped in July next
year over sea to Calais, or rather to Guines, where Sir
James Tyrell was then captain.   But Henry soon after,
sending two ambassadors to the Archduke Philip, instructed them in passing through Calais to use every
possible persuasion to induce him to return ; and their
arguments were so successful that he did come back, and
was again received into favour, insomuch that he followed
the king to Calais in 1500, and was present at his
meeting with the Archduke Philip.   But in August
next year, about three months before the marriage of
Prince Arthur, he escaped abroad again, along with his
brother Richard, and found his way to the Court of the
Emperor Maximilian in the Tyrol.   A sympathising
friend had informed the emperor that the Earl of Suffolk
meant to recover what he called his right to the Crown,
declaring that many of Henry's subjects were disgusted
with his "murders and tyrannies," which no doubt referred particularly to the death of Warwick and partly,
perhaps, to the extortions of Empson and Dudley.
And Maximilian, with his usual imprudence, had at
once declared that if Suffolk would only come to

him, he would assist him to obtain the object of his ambition.

The sympathising friend was Sir Robert Curzon, a man who lived many years afterwards, when he was restored to favour, in tolerably good repute, apparently, both with the king and with his successor Henry VIII. But at this time, and for a year or two afterwards, he was naturally under a cloud. He seems to have been a man of old chivalric feeling, and two years before Suffolk's flight he had obtained leave of the king to quit his post as Captain of Hammes Castle, near Calais, and fight against the infidels. He had accordingly given his services to Maximilian, whose territories were harassed by the Turk, and so highly were these esteemed that he was created by his new master a baron of the empire. It was probably owing to this that in his own country he was, in later days, frequently called Lord Curzon, for there is no record of his creation as an English peer. After a time he returned to England, and not only was his offence overlooked, but he received a pension of £400 a year from the Crown. Thus Henry had pretty good security that indignation at Warwick's execution would not tempt him to break his allegiance a second time.

It was thought by many, and is even stated in chronicles, that Curzon only played the part that Clifford had played before him, and that when, soon after Suffolk's second flight, the earl and he and five other persons were denounced at Paul's Cross as the king's enemies, it was only to give Suffolk the better assurance that his friend was not betraying him. I believe that this is a mistake, as I find that some persons

who stood security for Curzon's fidelity as Captain of
Hammes actually forfeited their recognisances four
years after Suffolk's flight; and so far as one can judge
of Curzon's character by later correspondence, he does
not seem to have been a double-dealer. Henry's suspicions, in fact, were seriously roused, and the chief friends
and near relations of Suffolk were immediately put
under arrest. These were his brother, Lord William
de la Pole; Lord William Courtenay, son of the Earl of
Devonshire, who had married his cousin Katharine,
daughter of Edward IV.; Sir James Tyrell, the Captain
of Guines, once the too faithful adherent of Richard
III.; and Sir John Wyndham. The suspicions against
the two Lords William seem to have arisen merely out
of their relationship to Suffolk and their connection with
the House of York. For this cause, although both were
imprisoned all Henry's days, Lord William Courtenay
was liberated on Herny VIII.'s accession, and the rigour
of Lord William de la Pole's confinement was relaxed.
But Sir James Tyrell and Sir John Wyndham were
executed for treason. The charge against the former,
of course, was for having received the Earl of Suffolk on
his first flight at Guines and given him some encouragement. But to obtain his arrest the whole army of
Calais had to besiege Guines Castle, and even then, it
was said, he only consented to come out on pledges for
his security in coming and going, which of course were
afterwards violated. He deserved, however, but little
pity. It does not seem to have been known till he was
condemned to die how deeply he was implicated (as an
accessory) in a much more grievous crime—the murder
of Edward V. and his brother.

These measures effectually prevented any outbreak at home. Henry's policy, besides, in requiring bonds and securities for every position of trust, joined to his continued watchfulness, naturally inclined all men who had anything to lose to become firm supporters of his government. Suffolk, on the other hand, had little reason to congratulate himself on the result of relying on Maximilian's promises. The emperor, indeed, received him as a kinsman, but hesitated at first to make good his word, on account of the amity between Henry and his son the archduke. Again, however, he would consider the matter carefully, and after keeping Suffolk at his Court for six weeks, he promised him the services of a German count with 4000 foot and 600 horse, and sent him to Aix-la-Chapelle with letters to the Council of that town to make further arrangements. The emperor also said he would obtain from Denmark shipping for an invading force. No effectual aid, however, was forthcoming. Repeated messages only brought new excuses for the non-fulfilment of imperial promises, till Maximilian was fain to suggest that Suffolk should apply to the King of France, or even endeavour to make peace with Henry, in which he promised to be his intercessor, seeing that he was about to make peace with Henry himself. He had good reason to do so, for on the day that he ratified the treaty he also signed an acquittance for a sum of £10,000, received from the King of England to enable him to maintain war against the Turks. Money was a thing Maximilian had always much difficulty in procuring, and for a substantial sum like this it was no wonder that he should undertake not to receive any English rebels henceforth.

The Spanish ambassador in Germany was also instructed by Ferdinand to press for Suffolk's expulsion
or extradition ; but the exile made a timely escape, and
after a vain effort to obtain assistance from the count
palatine, entered the territory of Gueldres with the view
of passing through it to George, Duke of Saxony, in
Friesland. He had by this time not only lost a fine
estate in England, but had been obliged to leave his
brother Richard behind him at Aix-la-Chapelle as a
hostage for payment of his debts. To crown all, in
Gelderland he was shut up in prison by the duke, and
only set at liberty on payment of 2000 florins, which a
Spanish merchant at Antwerp was found willing to
advance for him. He then, by the duke's connivance,
managed to collect a band of about 6000 foot, not
ostensibly under his leadership, The duke evidently
thought he could make use of him in some way, and if
he could do no more, compel the King of England to
pay a handsome price for his delivery. But in 1505, on
a peace being made between Gueldres and the Archduke
Philip, who had ere this become King of Castile by the
death of his mother Isabella, he was delivered up into
the hands of Philip ; and there we must leave him for
the present.

Henry's alliance with Spain, cemented by the marriage
of Arthur with Katharine, was not materially weakened
by the death of the former ; and though he declined to
comply with the demand for the restoration of the
dowry or to send Katharine back to Spain, he intended
to make the Spanish sovereigns feel quite as much as
heretofore that his interests were theirs. The retention
of Katharine in England gave him an advantage. Isa-

bella had proposed, as we have seen, her marriage with Prince Arthur's brother. But next year Henry, finding himself a widower, made a monstrous counter-proposal to marry her himself. It seems hardly conceivable in these days how the same man who had comforted his queen, and been comforted by her in their joint affliction on the death of their first-born, could, immediately on that queen's death, suggest anything so repulsive as a match with his own daughter-in-law. Not that, as regards mere affinity, it was worse than Katharine marrying her husband's brother; but it was an outrage upon nature both in respect to difference of age and the fact that Henry was now Katharine's natural protector. Isabella was deeply shocked, and was now more anxious than ever that even if a betrothal with the second son had been already concluded, Katharine should come home without more delay, for it was no longer honourable, she said, for her to remain in the country under such protection.

Still, it was obviously not an easy matter to get Katharine at once out of Henry's hands, and Isabella, to divert him from the project he had laid before her, suggested to him another match in place of it. The lady was a niece of her own, or rather of her husband's, Joanna, widow of Ferdinand II. of Naples, who was called the young Queen of Naples to distinguish her from her mother, another Joanna, widow of Ferdinand I. These two ladies lived together at Valencia. Henry did not reject the proposition, but kept it for some time under consideration. As to Katharine, however, he at last concluded a treaty for her marriage with his second son, in which the Spanish sovereigns renounced all claim

to re-demand the first instalment of her dowry, and promised to pay the remainder within ten days after the
new marriage should be solemnised. A special dispensation had to be procured from Rome for a case of so near
affinity, but after some delay a bull for the purpose was
sent to Spain to comfort Isabella, then on her deathbed.
She died on the 26th of November 1504.

Her death at once made a great change in the position
of Ferdinand—how great a change was at first a matter
of speculation. But it was clear that the kingdoms of
Castile and Arragon had only been united by his marriage
with Isabella ; so that by the order of descent the former
belonged now not to him, but to his daughter Joanna, the
wife of the Archduke Philip, and she would convey the
Crown to her husband.   Philip and Joanna were, in fact,
at once proclaimed King and Queen of Castile by Ferdinand's own orders ; but he still claimed a right to administer the kingdom and to receive its revenues while he
lived, in accordance with the will of Isabella, which had
been approved by the Cortez. For as to Joanna it was well
known that she was weak in mind and could not govern
except through her husband ; while Philip was a foreigner,
and could not be expected to understand the Spaniards.
Nevertheless several of the nobles of Castile were anxious
to emancipate themselves from Ferdinand's control, who
had persistently endeavoured, like Henry in England, to
depress their order ; and they kept up a correspondence
with Philip in the Low Countries, to induce him to
hasten his coming to his new kingdom.

All this Henry marked attentively, or was anxious to
inquire into.   So, as the Spanish sovereigns had for
some time been pressing for a new treaty of alliance

against France, he sent next year three gentlemen on a
special mission to Ferdinand, to deliver to him a copy
of his own proposals on that subject, and press for an
answer. But this was evidently a mere pretext, and not
the main object of their mission; which was to ascertain, in conversation with any Spanish grandees or statesmen they should come across, what authority the King
of Arragon now possessed in the realm of Castile, and
what degree of favour his subjects, especially the great
nobles, bore him; what likelihood there was of Philip
and Joanna's coming, and whether, if they came, Ferdinand's authority or theirs was likely to be most regarded;
also, whether he had secure hold of the realm of Naples.
In short, the ambassadors were to investigate as thoroughly as they could all the elements of Ferdinand's
strength and weakness. But they had also another set
of instructions, under which, making rather a circuitous
route to Ferdinand's Court, for which they made a
plausible excuse on their arrival, they paid a visit to
the young Queen of Naples at Valencia, collected information about her circumstances, and took a number of
observations about her stature, complexion, and the like,
in reply to a set of interrogatories by no means delicate,
which, however, showed Henry's extreme anxiety to be
fully informed as to her personal attractions. In these
matters the report was highly favourable. But her jointure in Naples was confiscated, and Henry soon turned
his thoughts another way.

Meanwhile he was taking good care not to allow
himself, as in days of old, to be bound to Ferdinand
more than Ferdinand was bound to him. Although it
had been arranged by treaty that the marriage of Henry,

Prince of Wales, and Katharine was to take effect as soon as the former attained the age of fourteen, provided only that it could be shown that the remaining instalments of the marriage portion were in London ready to be delivered, Henry, for still better security, caused his son to make a formal protest against the match as an arrangement made without his consent while he was under marriageable age, and which he did not mean to carry out. This protest was made before witnesses in a room in Richmond Palace, but no diplomatic use seems to have been made of it afterwards; it was evidently a thing which could be pleaded or withdrawn at will, and Henry had no occasion to resort to it. The money from Spain was not forthcoming, and Ferdinand only promised that he would send it when the prince was *fifteen* years complete, when he had previously intimated that it was to be paid a year earlier. Henry, however, had already received one-half and could afford to wait. Katharine was not so comfortable, for though Ferdinand had sent her to England with gold and jewels valued at 35,000 scudos, which was to make up part of the value of what was still to be paid, De Puebla was instructed for that very reason to see to its safe custody and not allow her to spend it. The result was that four years after her landing in England she complained that she had not had a single penny allowed her except for food. Her father apparently had determined to throw the burden of her support upon Henry, while Henry conceived that full provision ought to have been made for her by Ferdinand. And so she remained for years in a painful state of destitution, unable even to reward her attendants for their services and enable them to buy clothes.

Early in 1506 a great piece of good fortune fell in Henry's way. In January Philip and Joanna set sail from Zealand for their new kingdom of Castile. In the Channel they met with a violent storm, which dispersed their fleet and compelled them to land at Melcombe Regis, opposite Weymouth, in Dorsetshire. They could not but notify their case to Henry, who at once invited them to his Court, showed them every possible attention, invested Philip with the order of the Garter, and got him to sign a treaty of alliance and amity; in consequence of which a few days after Philip felt himself obliged to surrender the fugitive Earl of Suffolk into Henry's hands. It is said that he first extracted from Henry a promise to spare his life, and that Henry detained him in England until the prisoner was fetched from Flanders. The former statement appears to have some foundation in fact, though the treaty of alliance which he had signed compelled Philip to surrender all English rebels unconditionally; and Suffolk, being consigned to the Tower, remained there unharmed all Henry's days, but was beheaded early in the succeeding reign, apparently without any further trial. But the second statement is certainly wrong; for Philip took his leave of Henry at the beginning of March, and Suffolk was not brought over till the end of the month. His surrender, however, was but a small part of the advantages gained by Henry from Philip's landing on his coast. Another treaty was arranged before the two kings parted, although it was dated 30th April, some weeks after Philip had left England, for regulating commercial intercourse between Henry's subjects and the Flemings; which was so greatly to the advantage of the former that it was called in the Netherlands the *Intercursus Malus*, in contradistinction to the treaty of 1496, which was named the *Intercursus Magnus.*

Nor was this all. Henry had formed a design of marrying Philip's sister, the Archduchess Margaret, a widow of about seven-and-twenty, who had had two husbands already—the first (who has been mentioned before) Prince John of Spain, eldest son of Ferdinand and Isabella; the second Philibert, Duke of Savoy. Her father, Maximilian, had already sent a power to con-clude the marriage treaty, and the matter was conveni-ently settled in London between ambassadors of Maxi-milian, Philip, and Henry, while Philip was still in England. Now, as Philip had left Margaret behind him to take care of the Low Countries in his absence, this marriage would have placed the government of those countries in Henry's hands, besides putting at his dis-posal the lady's jointure alike in Spain and in Savoy. But Margaret herself showed decided opposition to it, and the project, though it was kept alive for years, was for a brief time dropped in favour of another matri-monial scheme which presently became possible by Philip's death, an event which took place in September following, only three months after his landing in Castile.

No sooner was this event known in England than Henry wrote to Ferdinand, with whom of course he was outwardly on the most amicable terms, offering to marry his widowed daughter Joanna. Henry doubtless knew very well that even before this time the lady had shown unmistakable symptoms of insanity; but that did not deter him from a political match which would have handed over to him the government of Castile. Such

being his aim, he could scarcely have expected Ferdinand
cordially to advance his suit, however willing he expressed
himself to do so, although he succeeded—shameful to
relate—in inducing Katharine to write to her father in
behalf of this unnatural project. For it seems that poor
Katharine saw no hope of relief from the poverty and
discomfort in which she lived except in the speedy
accomplishment of her own marriage, which she saw was
delayed by differences that had arisen between her father
and her father-in-law ; and she begged that her father
would at least humour the King of England until her
own interests were secured. But Ferdinand's ambassador, De Puebla, went even further ; he was convinced
that Henry would not interfere with Ferdinand's regency
in Castile, and suggested that the match would even be
for his master's interest, for if the lady's insanity were
incurable it would be just as well that she should live in
England, whereas, on the other hand, her best chance of
recovering from it would be by marriage with such a
king as Henry. And as for the view taken in England,
he wrote that none of the English councillors thought
much of her malady, as it was not of a kind to prevent
her bearing children !

Ferdinand, whatever his private opinion was, had
made no other objection to Henry's proposal than that
he was not sure if his daughter was inclined to marry
again at all ; if she did it should be with no other than
the King of England. But the project must be kept
quiet, for Joanna was wilful and not easily managed.
Henry no doubt saw that the game of excuses could
easily be carried on indefinitely in this case, and it would
seem that he was only trying to throw Ferdinand off his

guard while maturing other designs with the same object.
Joanna was not given up, but his old proposal to Margaret
of Savoy was pressed again, while at the same time he
distinctly told Katharine that he was no longer bound
to marry her to the Prince of Wales, seeing that her
father had failed to remit the marriage portion as stipulated in the treaty. The French king, he knew, would
be only too glad to offer the Prince of Wales the sister
of Francis, Duke of Angoulême—a match that had been
spoken about before; and Henry for his part started a
new project, which it was not in the power of Ferdinand
to interfere with, for a marriage between his daughter
Mary and Philip's son Charles, Prince of Castile, afterwards the great Emperor Charles V.

In connection with this marriage project Bacon
mentions a "tradition in Spain, though not with us,"
that Ferdinand, though the match was suggested by
himself originally, began to be jealous that Henry aspired
to the government of Castile, as administrator during
the minority of his son-in-law. But although he knew
that the nobles of Castile were impatient of Ferdinand's
government, Bacon thought it improbable that Henry
could have cherished a design so far-reaching and adventurous. Bacon, unfortunately, had not access to the
Spanish State papers of the period, or he would have
seen, as the reader has seen already, that this was not the
first project conceived by Henry which was likely to
have such a result. He would also have found pretty
sufficient evidence that, while friendly relations were still
maintained, Henry had lost much of his old regard for
Ferdinand; and probably he would have found reason to
believe that this was so even at the time of Philip's visit

to England. Indeed all the evidence we have relating
to that event tends to show that Henry, instead of being,
as Bacon informs us, merely polite to Philip, while
cordially maintaining his alliance with Ferdinand, was,
on the contrary, very cordial to Philip and merely polite
to Ferdinand. His experience of the King of Arragon
in past times had not been such as to inspire him with a
deep sense of gratitude, and if he did not actually seek
to supplant him in the government of Castile, he certainly
meant to show him how easily he could be supplanted.
There were, in fact, very alarming rumours spread abroad
in 'Spain that Henry not only intended to lay claim to
the government of Castile, but was collecting a fleet for
the purpose of landing in the country. Ferdinand himself, though he probably looked upon this as an exaggerated alarm, did not think it advisable to treat it
altogether with contempt, but raised troops and got ready
vessels to protect the coast. It is pitiful to think of the
straits and difficulties, the alarms and apprehensions, the
ignoble devices and diplomatic meanness to which the
once great King of Arragon had been reduced ever since
he lost his hold upon Castile by the death of Isabella.
For, first, to strengthen himself against Philip he had
quite reversed all his former policy. He had made an
alliance with France, married a French princess, and
bought off the French claims on Naples so as to have an
undivided sovereignty at least in southern Italy. Recalled to Spain by Philip's death, he did not find Castile
more manageable in consequence of what he had done.
He was in straits for money. He had probably (for his
excuse be it said) real difficulty in sending even the tardy
and inadequate remittances which he actually did send

to relieve his daughter in England from painful pecuniary embarrassment. But for a time he gave up all thoughts of fulfilling the necessary condition for the completion of her marriage by sending to England the second instalment of her dowry; and it was said he had even told the French king that he did not expect the marriage to come off at all.

Nor perhaps would he have done anything to advance it, whatever his daughter suffered, if he could have dealt with Henry as he dealt with Louis XII. It is recorded that, on hearing of a complaint made by the latter that he had cheated him once, Ferdinand promptly answered, "He lied, the drunkard! I cheated him three times." Such an achievement was to the Catholic king a highly creditable piece of diplomacy; but he could make no similar boast as regards Henry. He only succeeded in compelling the King of England for a time to relieve Katharine's urgent necessities, so that she was able, by Henry's help, to prevent her servants going about in rags. But it was no concern of Henry's to advance her marriage if Ferdinand did not fulfil the necessary terms. He seemed, in fact, to have had enough of Ferdinand's alliance, and to be cultivating that of Maximilian instead; for though he had not given up his suit for the hand of Joanna, he really cared nothing about it, and was renewing his old overtures to Margaret of Savoy, while the proposed match of Prince Charles of Castile with his daughter Mary was received with favour on both sides.

Matters, in fact, looked very serious for Ferdinand. Either of the two marriages which Henry had in view was against his interest; for the first would have put at the King of England's command the resources of the Low

Countries, the second the government of Castile. And
when to either or both of these advantages was to be
added the friendship, or even the neutrality of France,
it was clear that an alienated England would be a most
dangerous power. For though Maximilian and Louis
XII. were not on the best of terms, both seemed anxious
to retain Henry's friendship, and Henry was no less
anxious to preserve theirs. He therefore, notwithstanding his suit to Margaret of Savoy, gave no encouragement to her envoy, the Provost of Cassel, whom she
sent to England to demand his armed interposition to
protect Flanders from aggression on the part of France
and Gueldres. He thought Flanders would do better to
make peace with France, which was far too strong to be
successfully resisted ; but he told the Provost of Cassel
that he could suggest to the emperor a course much
more for his advantage, which would not only settle the
difficulty about Gueldres, but make him really the most
formidable potentate in Europe. For if Maximilian
would be guided by his advice he could show him how,
as guardian of his grandson Prince Charles, he might
wrest the administration of Castile out of Ferdinand's
hands. The mode in which this was to be done, he
intimated to the ambassador, was a thing which he could
not commit to paper : he would only confide it to Maximilian himself in secret at a personal interview. But
the emperor might be assured that he was not suggest-
ing anything impracticable, and he only wished that the
emperor never embarked on expeditions which had been
less carefully planned and considered beforehand than
this.

Words like these, coming from a king of Henry's

repute for wisdom, and addressed to such an ambassador
as George de Theimseke, Provost of Cassel—a statesman
of whose learning and judgment Sir Thomas More,
having had conferences with him a few years later in
the Netherlands, gives a very high estimate in his *Utopia*
—were not mere idle breath. The ambassador was
strongly impressed with the importance of the communication, although the plan which Henry had in view
was kept secret even from himself. He doubtless had
some faint surmises on the subject; and it is clear that
months before the conversation referred to, Ferdinand
himself had become keenly alive to the possibility of a
dangerous confederacy of other powers against him.
For in the first place Henry had made a league with
Maximilian and Prince Charles of Castile for mutual
defence (21st December 1507), and at the same time
had made a treaty for the marriage of Prince Charles to
his daughter Mary; and secondly, about the same time
Maximilian had made a league with France. Ferdinand
was evidently very much alarmed; and he at once sent
to England Gutierre Gomez de Fuensalida, one of the
ablest negotiators in Spain, with the remainder of the
money that was to be paid for the Princess Katharine's
dowry.

He anticipated, and with perfect justice, that Henry
had now so great an advantage over him as to be able to
dictate his own terms if the marriage was to take place
at all. For Henry refused to accept the money offered,
saying that he was no longer bound to take it in the
form originally agreed,—indeed he was no longer bound
by the treaty at all, since the time of payment stipulated
had so long gone by. And so one by one he wrung from

Ferdinand a number of concessions that he had refused
to make before. The whole of the dowry must be paid
in coin; it must be handed over to himself, and Ferdinand must absolutely renounce any such claim as he put
forward after Arthur's death to have it restored to him.
under any circumstances whatsoever. Finally, when
these two demands had been conceded, Henry insisted
that Ferdinand must ratify the treaty for the marriage
of Prince Charles and the Princess Mary*; otherwise the
marriage between the Prince of Wales and Katharine
would not even yet take place. In short, he must give
his sanction to the very means Henry was using to
supplant his government in Castile.

Ferdinand was intensely irritated. This last demand
was beyond endurance, but how it was to be met was
not an easy question even for so astute a diplomatist as
himself. His ambassador, Fuensalida, too, had an uncomfortable time of it, and complained that he was
treated with positive discourtesy at Henry's Court; while
his subjects at home were indignant that he should allow
his daughter to remain in England when no arrangement
was made for her living there under honourable conditions. Yet he durst not quarrel with Henry, and had
no means of fetching his daughter away without Henry's
consent. He must be on his guard, too, lest the King
of England should overreach him in diplomacy at foreign
Courts; for he could not but have uncomfortable suspicions as to what was going on there. He was, however,
tolerably sure of France; as for the needy Maximilian,
he was happily fickle, else so good a paymaster as Henry
would certainly have bound him fast in everything to
the interests of England. But Maximilian was at this

time led away by another weakness. He hated Venice, which the year before had given him an inglorious repulse in seeking to pass into Italy to receive his crown as emperor; and he fell a victim to the devices of the Cardinal d'Amboise, the wily minister of Louis XII., who was endeavouring to smooth the way for another descent on Italy by his master. The two rivals, in fact, were to make common cause. Venice had become in different ways offensive to them both; and they were coming to a secret agreement, in which Ferdinand of Arragon and the warlike Pope Julius II. were pledged to join them, to divide a considerable share of the Venetian territory among themselves.

It was no part of Henry's policy, even if he knew all that was going on, to meddle in any way with this iniquitous compact, which was finally concluded at Cambray on the 10th of December 1508. A treaty about Gueldres arranged at the same time served as a cloak for the more mischievous agreement. Henry had his own objects, which the selfishness and narrowness of the confederates rather assisted than hindered. But . he knew something of their doings, and it suited his own interests to give a word of advice beforehand to the principal dupe. Maximilian, indeed, never found a convenient opportunity for the personal interview Henry had proposed to him; but it is not unlikely that Henry, nevertheless, found the means of communicating either to him or to his daughter, Margaret of Savoy, a good part of the secret he had hinted at. For the English ambassador in the Low Countries, Sir Edward Wingfield, urged Margaret, who was to be the leading negotiator for the emperor at Cambray (the league, in fact, was

said to be her work, as the real author of it no doubt
desired it should be reputed), to endeavour as much as
possible to break up the alliance between Ferdinand and
the King of France, as that was the only thing which
enabled the former to maintain his hold upon Castile,
of which kingdom, if he had no longer such support, he
would be obliged to resign the government to Maximilian
as guardian for his infant grandson Prince Charles. Of
course if Maximilian, acting on such advice, had ever
really obtained the government of Castile, he would have
practically handed it over to his adviser Henry ; for, as
Bacon truly remarks with relation to this contingency,
"as for Maximilian, upon twenty respects he could not
have been the man."

There was another English envoy besides Wingfield
engaged in these delicate communications with the Archduchess Margaret. Henry had discovered before this
the marvellous diplomatic ability of Thomas Wolsey,
afterwards the great cardinal and for a long time sole
minister of his son. It seems to have been about this
time that he was sent on that memorable mission to
Flanders (Cavendish says to the emperor, then staying
at a short distance from Calais) which he accomplished
with such astonishing celerity as to have returned to
Richmond on the third night after his despatch. We
know at least that an envoy did return from Calais with
remarkable celerity in the beginning of August 1508,
and we know also that Wolsey was at Mechlin in October
engaged in negotiating not only for the king's marriage
with Margaret, but also for bringing the government of
Castile into Henry's hands. But this was not the first
time he had given proof of his diplomatic skill ; for in

the beginning of the same year Henry had sent him into
Scotland, where he had done excellent service in remon-
strating with the King of Scots, and at the same time
preventing a rupture with England which a French
faction there had been very anxious to promote. For
in 1505 James had solemnly promised that he would not
renew the old league with France against England, and
yet now, on some very slender pretext, he was on the
point of doing so, and last year he had sent an embassy
to France, consisting of the Earl of Arran and his brother
Sir Patrick Hamilton, who passed through England in
disguise to the Court of Louis XII. This irregularity
Henry would not allow them to repeat, but caused a
gentleman named Hugh Vaughan to meet them in Kent
on their return and conduct them up to London, where
they were detained for some time and not permitted to
pursue their journey home (though they were feasted
by the mayor and sheriffs, and allowed to visit the king
himself) until satisfactory explanations had been made,
and the peace of the two kingdoms thoroughly assured
by the result of Wolsey's mission.

His negotiations in Flanders do not seem to have
been quite so successful, though he acquitted himself in
that delicate mission entirely to Henry's satisfaction.
The despatches relating to them are so mutilated that
we cannot quite follow the whole course of the proceed-
ings ; but we find Wolsey complaining of the difficulty
of fixing the agents of Maximilian and his daughter to
their promises, so that real and substantial progress was
hardly to be looked for. Henry had been willing, if the
marriage could have been arranged, to reside at times in
the Low Countries for their more efficient government ;

or he would have agreed, if desired, that the administration should still be carried on in the name of Margaret only. He was willing to hear all objections, and to meet them in any reasonable way. But it was in vain to hope for anything definite from people who were perpetually changing their minds. Maximilian and his councillors were much more intent on concluding the secret league against Venice; and as to the policy of separating France and Arragon, the hint does not seem ever to have been taken up. Henry accordingly was left to pursue his own game.

But one thing was fixed already, and he did not mean to let slip his advantage there. The marriage between his daughter Mary and the Prince of Castile having been already arranged by treaty, Lord Berghes was sent over to England, on the part of Maximilian and Charles, to celebrate it by proxy; and so, after the manner of the times, the boy of eight was married to the girl of twelve (as far as such a thing could be) with great rejoicings and celebrations in London, where the event was looked upon as the confirmation of an old and lasting friendship, bringing the royal line of England once more into close relations with the house of Austria. The celebration took place at Richmond on the 17th of December—just a week after the secret treaty against Venice had been concluded at Cambray. Four days later—it deserves to be noted how the wheels were greased—the agents of Maximilian and Prince Charles handed over to Henry in pawn a jewel called "the rich *fleur-de-lis*" for a sum of 50,000 crowns in gold. Nobody ever settled anything with Maximilian without ready money.

Even this proxy marriage must have been a bitter pill to Ferdinand ; for Henry was still to all appearance on the way to win and wrest Castile out of his hands. But it was not to be ; for the enemy whom none can resist was now close upon Henry's footsteps, and he had but four months to live.

CHAPTER XIII

CONCLUSION

HENRY'S health, never very strong, had been for some
time perceptibly declining, though the energy with
which he attended to business seemed hardly diminished
by his accumulated infirmities. Indeed his spirits rose
so much above his bodily frailty that for a time in 1507
he seemed positively robust after a long illness, hunting
and hawking with as much zest as if he had been twenty
years younger. But he had now begun to be attacked
with gout. He had also pains in the chest and difficulty
of respiration. Having a presentiment of his approaching end, he became more than usually liberal in alms-
giving. He discharged the debts of all persons imprisoned in London for sums under forty shillings. He
expressed remorse for the severities practised under his
authority by Empson and Dudley, and it must have
been owing to his dying injunction and for the repose
of his soul that many of the bonds obtained by them
were cancelled at the commencement of the succeeding
reign. Law, however, was one thing and conscience
another. Empson and Dudley were allowed to go on
to the last with extortions which had only a show of
legality to justify them, and were sacrificed to popular

indignation as soon as the eighth Henry succeeded his father.

Henry also finished the hospital of the Savoy the year before his death, and made provision for the splendid chapel at Westminster in which he lies interred. His taste in building was magnificent. The wealth he had amassed and left behind him, locked up in various secret places, was reported to have amounted to nearly £1,800,000, a sum probably equal in value to £18,000,000 at the present day. Yet he was far from miserly. He valued money only for money's worth; and to him a large reserve was a great guarantee for peace and security. He made, moreover, a princely use of his wealth, encouraged scholarship and music as well as architecture, and dazzled the eyes of foreign ambassadors with the splendour of his receptions.

As a king, Bacon tells us that he was "a wonder for wise men." Few indeed were the councillors that shared his confidence, but the wise men, competent to form an estimate of his statesmanship, had but one opinion of his consummate wisdom. Foreigners were greatly struck with the success that attended his policy. Ambassadors were astonished at the intimate knowledge he displayed of the affairs of their own countries. From the most unpropitious beginnings, a proscribed man and an exile, he had won his way in evil times to a throne beset with dangers; he had pacified his own country, cherished commerce, formed strong alliances over Europe, and made his personal influence felt by the rulers of France, Spain, Italy, and the Netherlands as that of a man who could turn the scale in matters of the highest importance to their own domestic welfare. It is true that he was

P

not taken into counsel in the iniquitous league of Cambray; but the matter did not concern England, and
since his advice was neglected by the only power that
he tried to warn, he was content to let it alone.   He
could afford to let such an alliance form itself and fall to
pieces, as it did very shortly after he was dead.

From first to last his policy was essentially his own ;
for though he knew well how to choose the ablest councillors, he asked or took their advice only to such an
extent as he himself deemed expedient.   In all his reign
he never removed a councillor except Sir William
Stanley; yet he allowed none of them to exercise any
predominant influence with him, but kept all the strings
of government in his own hand.   "He was of an high
mind and loved his own will and his own way, as one
that revered himself and would reign indeed . . . not
admitting any near or full approach, either to his power
or to his secrets."   No one can understand his reign, or
that of his son, or, we might add, of his granddaughter
Queen Elizabeth, without appreciating the fact that,
however well served with councillors, the sovereign was
in those days always his own Prime Minister.   Not even
Wolsey, whose wonderful ability the seventh Henry was
the first to discover, could for one moment lead the
eighth, as men supposed, in a way that the eighth Henry
himself had not distinctly considered and approved
before he took it.   The Tudor policy all along was for
the sovereign to "reign indeed"—or, in modern language, not only to reign but to govern.   Yet so much
of what we call constitutional principle was always
admitted by these princes, that their ministers and not
themselves were responsible for anything done amiss.

Morton and Bray might be exposed to popular oppro-brium for the severity of impositions which they had really tried to mitigate. No one could be so disloyal as to reproach the king himself, and no minister could re-lieve himself of blame by declaring what he had said at the Council table. It was a minister's duty, in short, to endure quietly unmerited reproach.

Not that the members of Henry's Council were by any means ciphers; for if that had been the case they would have served him ill. On the contrary, it was noted by a shrewd observer at the time that they really exercised a considerable control over him. He had lived so much abroad that he was only half an English-man, and it was apparent to those who were behind the scenes that he would have preferred to govern England in the French fashion if he could. He really needed advisers who could bring him into harmony with the national sentiment, and he yielded to them such careful deference as might enable him to fix responsibility on those by whom he had been chiefly led. But he was less under control towards the end of his reign, when it must be owned that, as he felt himself more secure in his seat, he yielded to viler influences, and became un-popular in consequence. And though he removed no councillor, it was known that one or two had distinctly lost their influence over him; while in some things, such as the employment of foreigners in the service of the State, he took a more liberal view himself than he felt it safe to follow.

Even the legislation of the reign must be regarded as in large measure due to Henry himself. We have no means, it is true, of knowing how much of it originated in his own mind; but that it was all discussed with him in Council and approved before it was passed we have every reason to believe. For he never appears to have put the royal veto upon any Bill, as constitutional usage both before and after his days allowed. He gave his assent to all the enactments sent up to him for approval, though he sometimes added to them provisos of his own. And Bacon, who knew the traditions of those times, distinctly attributes the good legislation of his days to the king himself. "In that part both of justice and policy which is the most durable part, and cut, as it were, in brass or marble, the making of good laws, he did excel." This statement, with but slight variations in the wording, appears again and again throughout the History; and elsewhere it is said that he was the best lawgiver to this nation after Edward I.; also that his laws, if carefully examined, "are deep and not vulgar; not made upon the spur of a particular occasion for the present, but out of providence for the future, to make the estate of his people still more and more happy, after the manner of the legislators in ancient and heroical times."

These observations, indeed, have not passed without criticism, and possibly some instances of what Bacon would have called the "deep" legislation might have gone, according to his own classification, under the name of "vulgar," or at least, if not intended to meet "a particular occasion," might have been distinctly traced to a widespread feeling in the community of some great public wants. Of such "vulgar" legislation Bacon himself admits that there was not a little, and a full examination of the subject would carry us beyond the limits of a volume like the present. The Parliaments, indeed, that Henry summoned were only seven in number, and seldom did any one of them last over a year, so that during a reign of nearly twenty-four years many years passed away without a Parliament at all. But even in those scanty sittings many Acts were passed to meet evils that were general subjects of complaint, such as the riots caused by the customs of livery and maintenance; to check collusive informations and other irregularities which vitiated the administration of justice in the country; to encourage complaints against justices of the peace, and provide for their being examined; to encourage in various ways manufactures and commerce, and to arrest what was much complained of, the depopulation of the country, due, as it was thought, to enclosures and the pulling down of dwelling-houses to enlarge sheep pastures. The modes in which it was attempted to meet the evils dealt with were frequently such as the political economy of our day would hardly approve; but even here we seem to see an advance upon previous times, if not even a higher degree of thoughtfulness than we meet with in succeeding reigns. As regards, for instance, the arrest of depopulation, there was a judicious avoidance of prohibition. The Act, indeed, required existing houses of husbandry to be kept up on pain of forfeiture of the land about them; but it did not insist on tillage or absolutely forbid enclosures.

There were also Acts to restrain the power of corporations to make by-laws inconsistent with the general good; to bring gaols throughout the country under the complete control of the sheriffs; to encourage shipping by requiring that wines and woads of Gascony and

Languedoc should be imported in English bottoms; to forbid as useless luxuries the importation of silk articles, such as ribbons and the like, from abroad; and further, to encourage the woollen manufactures of the kingdom, and at the same time—a clearly erroneous policy—to regulate the prices of the different kinds of wool; also to keep gold within the kingdom by forbidding payments to foreigners in that metal.

In his last Parliament, which met in the nineteenth year of his reign, an Act was passed for the reform of the coinage, which had been very much clipped and counterfeited, and it was well known throughout the kingdom that Henry himself was the chief instigator of the measure, and that it was he who gave most thought to the remedy in the calling in of the vitiated currency and the issuing of a better. In this as in other things no doubt he took care of his own profit, for the mint was a large gainer by the exchange; but none the less did he do an important service to the mercantile community at large.

That Henry was a lover of peace at all times is proved by the whole history of his reign and all that we know of his negotiations. This was naturally his policy, because even when he grew more secure he had nothing to gain by war, but much to lose, and in the beginning of his reign peace was to him the only way of safety. That he "trafficked," as Bacon says, in the war with France, and thereby deceived his subjects—for his own advantage, it is true, but for their best interests as well—ought hardly to be imputed to him as a fault. The thing was really forced upon him by the necessities of his position. At least it may be questioned in this point

whether Bacon does not judge him too harshly in saying
that he loved "a noise of war" to draw forth treasure,
as well as a peace to coffer it up; for the noise of war
was none of his making. Like all great statesmen of
early times, he was quite above the mere national prejudice that was always ready to kindle the flames against
France; and shortly before his death he recommended
his son and successor to pursue the same policy as himself. By preserving friendship with France and amass-
ing money he told him that he would be best able to
preserve his kingdom in peace and break the power of
faction if it ever became dangerous.

But, apart from policy, his love of peace was probably
due, like his clemency as a ruler, to his own natural
disposition, though in both cases it was a politic clemency.
He made rebellions, like wars, pay their own expenses,
and even yield him a mine of treasure, which was a
source, in its turn, of stability to the country, giving
him more ample power to put down future outbreaks.
For the great majority of insurgents he had no other
punishment than fines; very few were put to death,
even among the nobility, towards whom he was more
severe than towards the common people. Respect for
law was upheld in the same way, as the Earl of Oxford
found to his cost when he received the king himself
with a number of men in livery, which the statute
forbade. Violation, even of laws which were antiquated,
was visited with fines which went to the king's coffers.
These things and the heavy taxation imposed upon the
people made his ministers very unpopular; but they were
more tolerable than the attainders and legal butcheries
which formed such a hideous feature in the reign of his son.

Another point as regards the mildness of his government is that he gave no encouragement to informers except such as he had specially commissioned to worm out the secrets of a dangerous conspiracy. Of disaffection and disloyalty among his subjects he probably knew at all times much more than he cared to notice ; but when anything was specifically reported to him he at once insisted on the informer giving up the source of his information, even if he pleaded that he was bound by oath to secrecy. He would either have nothing said at all or dive to the very bottom of the subject, and take care that no danger should ever come to a head.

It is also well remarked by his biographer that "he had nothing in him of vainglory, but yet kept state and majesty to the height, being sensible that majesty maketh the people bow, but vainglory boweth to them." This stateliness, keeping just a sufficient distance between the sovereign and the subject, was in marked contrast with the policy of the House of York; for both Edward IV. and Richard III. had always lowered themselves somewhat in courting popularity. Yet it is a mistake to suppose that he was severe and ungenial. The sweetness of his expression seems to have charmed the citizens of York at the very commencement of his reign, and we have several indications besides of a kindly, pleasant, affable, and even humorous disposition. Once, after listening to an elaborate address, he asked Fitzsimons, Archbishop of Dublin, what he thought of the orator's performance. "Excellent," said the archbishop, "saving that I think he flattered your Majesty too much." "In good faith," replied Henry, "we were greatly of that opinion ourselves." Another anecdote, also of an address made to him, shows ready wit as well as humour in the reply. John de Giglis, Bishop of Worcester, having called him " pastor " in a Latin poem stuffed full no doubt of the elaborate classical compliments then in vogue, the king rejoined impromptu, probably in the very same metre—

> " Si me pastorem, te decet esse pecus."

It may be that these touches of humour were compara- tively rare ; but he was always a ready and pleasing speaker, and it was certainly well known that at times at least he could be very genial. Bacon tells us that at tournaments and other spectacles " he was rather a princely and gentle spectator than seemed much to be delighted." Yet once at a tournament when, as a sort of interlude between more serious challenges, two riders were commanded to run a course with spears, they both decked their horses fantastically in paper, the one "in manner of a barde," and the other " of a demi-trapper," the latter with ridiculous devices painted upon it " to cause the king to laugh." But the reader has seen already how he could unbend in the amusing interview with Kildare related in a previous chapter. However grave habitually, he was anything but sour or surly. He spoke French fluently and had a competent knowledge of Latin, but was unable to read Spanish. He commonly addressed ambassadors in French, and enjoyed French literature more than any other. He could scarcely be called a learned man, yet he was a lover of learning, and gave his children an excellent education. His Court was open to scholars, and even his nursery was visited once by More and Erasmus, when the future Henry VIII., then a boy of nine, solicited from the famous Dutchman, by a note penned in the middle of his dinner, some contribution from his pen. We may be pretty sure that even the seventh Henry was not destitute of that taste for literature which was so marked a feature in the character of his son.

It is further remarked by the great philosopher who wrote his history, as a thing which tended to make him absolute but did not promote his own security, that he loved to promote clergymen and lawyers. By the traditions of English government a king ought to have been easily accessible to the advice of his nobility, and it does not appear that he despised good counsel even from them when he could get it. But on the whole the lay nobles were not such acute statesmen as he could find in the ranks of the clergy; and many of them required careful looking after lest they should stir up disorder. He could, moreover, reward clergymen for their services by good livings, without imposing any charge on the royal treasury; while lawyers, on the other hand, were bound to give him professional advice when wanted, as they naturally looked to the king for promotion.

Whether he was in the habit of conversing with churchmen on religious subjects we do not know; but he was certainly religious after the fashion of his day. His feeling towards a crusade has already been referred to. His religious foundations and bequests perhaps do not necessarily imply anything more than conventional feeling. But we must not overlook the curious circumstance that he once argued with a heretic at the stake at Canterbury and got him to renounce his heresy. It is melancholy to add that he did not thereupon release him from the punishment to which he had been sentenced; but the fact seems to show that he was afraid of encouraging insincere conversions by such leniency. During the last two or three years of the fifteenth century there was a good deal of procedure against heretics, but on the whole, we are told, rather by penances than by fire. Henry had no desire to see the old foundations of the faith disturbed. His zeal for the Church was recognised by no less than three Popes in his time, who each sent him a sword and a cap of maintenance; and I doubt not that he looked on the cause of the Church as closely connected with the stability of his own government. It was so, indeed, even where the Church's ancient rights were qualified, as in the case of sanctuaries, through his influence at the Court of Rome; for he obtained from Innocent VIII. some restriction of their ancient privileges, which greatly checked a multitude of abuses.

To commerce and adventure he was always a good friend. By his encouragement Sebastian Cabot sailed from Bristol and discovered Newfoundland—the New Isle, as it at first was called. Four years earlier Columbus had first set foot on the great western continent, and had not his brother been taken by pirates at sea, it is supposed that he too might have made his great discovery under Henry's patronage.

THE END